C000257275

THE
BLACK
SCIENCE

To Agnes Shifferly and Shirley Marsee
To Bo Wall and C.J. Grodek

THE
BLACK
SCIENCE

ANCIENT AND MODERN TECHNIQUES OF NINJA MIND MANIPULATION

DR. HAHA LUNG

CHRISTOPHER B. PROWANT

PALADIN PRESS · BOULDER, COLORADO

Also by Dr. Haha Lung
The Ancient Art of Strangulation
Assassin!: The Deadly Art of the Cult of the Assassins
Knights of Darkness: Secrets of the World's Deadliest Night Fighters
Shadowhand: The History and Secrets of Ninja Taisavaki (with Christopher B. Prowant)

The Black Science: Ancient and Modern Techniques of Ninja Mind Manipulation
by Dr. Haha Lung and Christopher B. Prowant

Copyright © 2001 by Dr. Haha Lung and Christopher B. Prowant

ISBN 1-58160-262-6
Printed in the United States of America

Published by Paladin Press, a division of
Paladin Enterprises, Inc.
Gunbarrel Tech Center
7077 Winchester Circle
Boulder, Colorado 80301 USA
+1.303.443.7250

Direct inquiries and/or orders to the above address.

Visit our Web site at www.paladin-press.com

TABLE OF CONTENTS

INTRODUCTION

> "Knowing your own mind is only half
> the battle. The other half is discerning
> the mind-set of your enemy;
> his motivation and his weakness."
> —Dirk Skinner,
> *Street Ninja: Ancient Secrets for
> Surviving Today's Mean Streets*

From fictional characters such as Svengali in George du Maurier's 1884 *Trilby* and Dr. Hannibal Lecter in *The Silence of the Lambs*, to real life manipulators such as Russia's Grigori Rasputin and America's Charlie Manson, nothing is more frightening (and fascinating) than the image of an evil mastermind capable of controlling—and even killing—others by simply using the power of his mind. These people are mind-slayers—individuals who have studied the human psychology and use it against those they would dominate.

From the 1950s up through the '70s, the U.S. government spent millions for the secret CIA-directed programs known as MK (for mind control) and MK-ULTRA, both of which were designed to develop mind-control weapons and strategies. Out of these programs came mind-control weapons ranging from "psychotronic" brainwashing devices to human mind weapons —psychic assassins capable of reading the enemy's mind and, ultimately, using their thoughts to kill the enemy from a distance.

These experiments and expenditures were justified under the argument that the U.S. government had to keep pace with similar mind-manipulation research being done by communist governments.

Don't laugh. It is a matter of public record that your tax dollars went to pay for this research.

Even now, years after these programs were acknowledged by our government and officially discontinued, stories continue to filter out of

Washington about mind-manipulation schemes and scenarios still being hatched in corporate boardrooms and seedy backrooms; mind-manipulation experiments played out at cult compounds in such out of the way places as Guyana and Waco, Texas.

To many Americans, the very idea of using mind manipulation goes against the chivalrous "Code of the West" and seems an affront to the memory of John Wayne standing tall, looking a bad guy in the eye.

Other more realistic and perhaps less sadistic voices ask "What is more humane, the indiscriminate use of a sledgehammer war strategy like carpet bombing—resulting in the deaths of thousands of innocents—or a scalpel-like incision targeting a single evil dictator?"

How much more effective and efficient, then, if we were somehow able to remove such a nemesis with a single thought?

Down through the ages unscrupulous individuals, self-serving cults, and various cadres of killers—from ancient Chinese magician-spies to medieval Middle Eastern assassins to the infamous ninja of Japan—have experimented with and applied a multitude of methods for controlling and killing their enemies by attacking their foes not on a physical battleground, but on a mental killing field.

These "mind-dancing" strategies and tactics range from the feasible to the far-fetched, from ancient voodoo to modern virtual reality.

Why should we take the time out of our busy schedules to study these ancient and modern mind-manipulation techniques?

Consider this:

Today Madison Avenue spends billions to influence us to buy things we don't need, to ensure our brand loyalty and, more insidious still, to lure us into supporting political candidates with slippery zippers.

This latter campaign goes hand-in-hand with governments and mega-corporations worldwide spending billions on psy-ops (psychological operations) designed to undermine the morale of their enemies while engendering patriotism and unquestioning obedience in their own people.

When this sort of mind manipulation is done by rival governments or rival religions, we call it propaganda and cult indoctrination. When we do it we call it advertising and public service announcements.

Studying traditional and current mind-manipulation strategies and techniques should not stem simply from our healthy paranoia about out-of-control government agencies constantly on the prowl for new ways to control people. Studying these techniques will help us guard ourselves and our loved ones against an endless array of criminal con men, crazed cult leaders, and opportunistic politicians.

Any realistic modern survival and self-defense training must include strategies for defending our own mind castles against intrusion. Thus, it is vital we master the art of mind-dancing for both defense and offense— before our enemies do.

Perhaps you believe yourself to be one of the favored few who don't have any enemies. Someone once said that Satan's greatest trick was convincing the world he doesn't exist. Perhaps the enemy you don't have has already mastered the techniques in this book!

"To subdue an enemy without fighting is the greatest of skills."
—Sun Tzu

CHAPTER 1

MASTERS OF THE GAME

"Ethereal and subtle, the master strategist
passes by without leaving a trace.
Mysterious, like the way of Heaven,
he passes by without a sound.
In this way master an enemy's fate."

—Sun Tzu

Of all the various cadres down through history to use mind manipulation as a weapon, hands down the most adept were the ninja of Japan.

Drawing on ancient texts and tactics from East Indian strategists and Chinese spies, medieval Japanese ninja further refined these techniques of mind manipulation before passing them down to us today.

THE ASIAN MIND

Experts disagree as to when and where the craft of Japanese *ninjutsu* (art of the ninja) actually began.

It is known that many Japanese ninja practices, including their mind-manipulation tactics and techniques, can be found with the mysterious Thuggee cult of India.[1]

Ancient India, the "mother" of civilization, produced many classics of military strategy, most of which contained at least passing reference to the importance of discerning—and then destroying—an enemy's mind-set. For example, the ancient Hindu text *Arthasastra* contained advice on the art of espionage and mind manipulation, as did the writings of Indian strategist Kautilya.

Other portions of Japanese ninja strategy can be traced back to ancient China's Warring States Period (453-221 BCE) when ruthless rival princes routinely employed subterfuge, spies, and mind manipulation to further their ambitions.

It was during this tumultuous period that the greatest of Asian strategists Sun Tzu wrote his *Ping Fa* (*Art of War*).

Sun Tzu's treatise is one of the first military books to carry a chapter devoted specifically to the use of secret agents. This masterpiece covers all aspects of warfare and includes extensive comments on how to gain insights into the strengths and weaknesses of an enemy's mind and how to wield those revelations during psychological warfare.

Sun Tzu understood that discerning the mind-set and motivations of an enemy was the first step in overcoming that enemy:

> "Know the enemy and know yourself and in a
> hundred battles you will never be in danger."

So insightful were Sun Tzu's observations that *Art of War* is more popular today than ever and has been applied to a wide variety of fields, not the least of which are Asian politics and finance.

China's Warring States Period also saw the emergence of several groups of specialized secret agents and assassins, the most feared of which were magician-like spies known as *moshuh nanren* (often referred to in hindsight as "the ninja of China").

Moshuh nanren were masters of espionage, assassination, and mind manipulation.

For example, moshuh nanren purposely cultivated an atmosphere of superstition and fear around themselves and their skullduggery. They did this through use of intimidation—their enemies disappearing in the middle of the night or found dead from the *dim-mak* (death touch) without any marks on them—and through encouraging the belief that moshuh nanren were descended from mythical *lin kuei* (forest demons).

Centuries later, Japanese ninja would use this same tactic, encouraging the belief that they were descended from mythical tengu demons.

Sun Tzu's *Art of War* was first "officially" introduced into Japan in the 8th century CE.

However, many moshuh nanren espionage techniques filtered into Japan between the 1st and 5th centuries, a period that saw a large influx of Chinese

Buddhists into Japan. Undoubtedly, Sun Tzu's *Art of War* came along for the ride. In addition to Sun Tzu, early Japanese strategists may have also studied other notable Chinese writers, for example Wu Ch'i (430-381 BCE):

> "One man willing to throw away his life
> is enough to terrorize a thousand."

Another influential Chinese strategist was Tu Mu (803-852 CE), who wrote extensively on the proper recruitment and employment of spies and double agents, especially individuals gleaned from an enemy's own country. Tu Mu's keen insight into the workings of the human mind detailed various ways disgruntled and disaffected individuals could be seduced into becoming traitors and double agents.

We can only speculate to what degree each of these Chinese, and to a lesser extent East Indian strategists, had on the development of the mind-manipulation tactics and techniques of medieval Japanese ninja. We do know for certain that, in short order, the ninja of Japan become quite adept at employing a myriad of mind-manipulation strategies, most of which remain valid today.

THE NINJA MIND

> "A keen insight into human psychology and predictability has always
> proven the ninja's greatest weapon. This remains true today."
> —Dirk Skinner

Japanese "ninja" techniques did not come into their own until the 6th century when Prince Shotoku, contestant for the imperial throne, recruited a *yamabushi* (mountain warrior-monk) by the name of Otomo-No-Saijin as a spy.

Where Otomo acquired his espionage skills and insight into human nature is not known. What is known is that Otomo was certainly adept at his craft, and instrumental in helping Shotoku outthink his enemies. Otomo's alias was Shinobi (one who sneaks in). The word ninja comes from the Japanese written character for shinobi and refers generically to anyone who uses stealth and subterfuge techniques (e.g. mind-manipulation) to accomplish his goals.

Over the next few centuries, Japanese techniques of espionage, sub-terfuge, and psychological warfare continued to be refined. In the 14th cen-tury, Japan was ripped end-to-end by savage internecine warfare between rival samurai clans. The savagery of this period stimulated an increase in "ninja" activity, as "ninja" criminal bands took advantage of the chaos to rob and plunder, and every freelance "ninja" spy peddled information on oppos-ing forces. Any act of savagery or subterfuge occurring during this time was attributed to "ninja," a catchall term not indicative of the later great orga-nized ninja clans. However, the 14th century did see the scattering of seeds that would eventually grow into true ninja clans in central Japan.

Eventually more than 50 shinobi-ninja clans—including the powerful Hattori, the Momochis and the Fijibayashis—would forge an almost autonomous state in the central provinces of Iga and Koga.

Insulated by dense forests, these shinobi-ninja perfected their stealth and intelligence-gathering craft, their martial arts, and, most importantly, their *satsujin-jutsu* (insights into the minds of men), both their own and that of potential enemies. As they grew more powerful, many of these shinobi clans were content to be left to themselves.

Other ninja clans, however, openly defied and actively warred against local daimyo (samurai overlords). More often than not they played one samurai clan against the other. This was sound ninja strategy. The more the daimyo warred amongst themselves—thinning their samurai ranks—the less manpower they had on hand to devote to hunting down ninja.

In the mid-1500s, Shogun Oda Nobunago and his two generals, Ieyasu Tokugawa and Hideyoshi Toyotomi launched a campaign to wipe out defiant ninja clans in central Japan. In his zeal, Nobunago drew no distinction between defiant ninja clans and those shinobi folk merely wanting to be left to themselves. This indiscriminate slaughter by Nobunago alienated many of the shinobi clans that might have otherwise not actively warred against him.

In November 1581, Nobunago's army invaded Iga province in force, decimating the shinobi clans. Those shinobi escaping immediate death during the intense fighting were hunted down and killed. A few clan leaders had read the writing on the wall and had made contingency plans for their peo-ple to escape to other parts of Japan, many to Kii province where still-defi-ant Buddhists had set up an enclave.

Not long after his invasion of Iga, Nobunago was assassinated by one of his own men, the Daimyo Akechi. Some say Akechi, a devout Buddhist, had simply had enough of Nobunago's persecution of peaceful Buddhists. Others whispered that the daimyo had fallen under the spell of ninja mind-masters.

Following the death of Nobunago, his general Hideyoshi Toyotomi seized power.

By 1590, Toyotomi, a commoner, had succeeded where all the emperors, shoguns, and daimyo before him hadn't, uniting the whole of Japan under his banner. Toyotomi began his rise to power as a juvenile henchman for a group of ruthless "ninja" highwaymen. From there, he manipulated his way into Nobunago's confidence; first as a valuable spy, then as an accomplished strategist, and eventually co-commander of Nobunago's forces.

Not surprisingly, the whispers were that "the ninja" Toyotomi had engineered Nobunago's death.

How ironic that Toyotomi, a man who owed his rise to ultimate power to ninja mind-manipulation tactics and techniques, would be the same man who would spell the beginning of the end of the great ninja clans.

Just as warring between rival samurai clans in the 14th century helped foster the development of ninjutsu, conversely Toyotomi's unification of Japan—and the resultant end to internecine fighting between lesser samurai lords—heralded the decline of overt ninja rebellion.

The emergence of a strong central government authority that local daimyo could call on for assistance against defiant clans helped spur the development of more covert methods of ninja craft, particularly in areas of mind manipulation.

As government, military, and law-enforcement became more centralized, most of the smaller, purely criminal "ninja" gangs dispersed. Others however remained defiant, forming larger criminal leagues and helping foster the emergence of the *yakuza*, Japan's version of the Mafia.

Ironically, still other ninja became policemen or became operatives for the centralized military's intelligence network. These converted operatives lent their ninja expertise (especially mind-manipulation techniques) to the creation of the Japanese military's feared *Kenpeitai* (Thought Control Bureau) and to the national *Tokko* (Thought Police). Established in 1911 to suppress left-wing movements in Japan, the Tokko's power continued to expand up through World War II when it specialized in enforcing thought-control policies of the pre-World War II militarist regime.

In the 17th century, the proper Tokugawa regime that succeeded Toyotomi's reign made it a capital offense to even say the word "ninja" since merely acknowledging the existence of such rogues challenged the very nature of rigid Japanese social structure. In their enemies' eyes, ninja had no honor because they used every manner of skullduggery to accomplish their goals. Where samurai fought face-to-face, adhering to the strict ideal of bushido chivalry, ninja were bound by no such rules of engagement, preferring instead to strike from behind or from afar.

What frightened proper Japanese society in general, and pretentious samurai in particular, was that ninja did not stop at unconventional physical warfare. Ninja also used psychological attacks, targeting their enemy where that enemy was most vulnerable and least able to defend themselves—through their secret lusts, inner fears, and superstitions.

More insidious still, you never knew when a wily ninja mind manipulator might succeed in "overshadowing" your brother, your wife, even your priest—any one of whom could slip a dirk into your back or poison into your cup while under the control of an accomplished ninja mind-wizard!

Progressing through the nine training halls of ninjutsu craft, students are quick to learn that for every one physical way to attack an enemy, there are 10 ways to attack his mind.

The Nine Training Halls

Each of the traditional Nine Halls of Ninjutsu contains a distinct field of training. While complete in and of themselves, by necessity each training hall compliments the other eight.

Ninja students are first given an overall course of training to familiarize them with all nine training halls. Students showing aptitude in a particular hall of study are then encouraged to specialize in that hall. In general, this nine halls regimen progresses from purely physical skills toward more mental skills, and culminates in the development of mental strategies and tactics designed to defeat a ninja's enemies without the danger of physical confrontation.

Even when the course of study appears to be purely physical in nature however, underlying the physical lesson is a valuable psychological principle to be mastered.

A brief overview of the nine halls:

Unarmed Combat

Teaches the student various systems of unarmed martial arts. Yet even this purely physical level of training contains a vital mental component. That is, hall instructors at this level are careful to note any psychological impediments or flaws in temperament in their students that might interfere with that student's mastery of physical skills.

Combat with Wooden Weapons

Allows the ninja student to augment his unarmed combat skills with natural wooden weapons provided by his environment, such as the *bo*-staff, *jo*-fighting sticks, or *nunchaku*.

Combat with Bladed Weapons

Familiarizes the student with a wide variety of bladed weapons, such as swords, knives, kama-sickles, and shuriken throwing stars.

Combat with Flexible Weapons

Introduces students to weapons such as chains, ropes, and even the innocuous scarf. Psychologically, at this level students learn that most valuable of lessons: Flexible weapons and tactics often succeed where more rigid tactics fail.

Specialized Combat Training

Requires the student to integrate the weapons and tactics learned in the four preceding halls with the use of specially-crafted shinobi devices and tactics. Note: Most ninjutsu schools draw a distinction between the first five halls, viewed as primarily physical in nature, and the following four, which emphasize mental acuity.

The Art of Disguise

Requires a study of physical make-up (wigs, prosthetics, dress, etc.) as well as other skills designed to allow the ninja to insert themselves into various roles. More than any other, this hall of study demands that students understand the psychology of others (such as their mind-set and cultural and religious traditions) in order to successfully perfect their role-playing.

The Art of Espionage

This hall first concerns itself with gathering intelligence and insight into the movements and motivation of foes. Ninja then use this information to devise a strategy for removing any obstacles blocking the ninja's objectives.

The traditional ninja way of thinking is that human obstacles can be overcome either through education or assassination. Despite their blood-thirsty reputation, shinobi-ninja always preferred "educating" an enemy (through the use of mental manipulation) rather than having to resort to physical methods of removing that enemy.

The Art of Escape and Evasion

Teaches the student *taisavak*i avoidance techniques ranging from physical skills (camouflage, locksmithing, escapology, etc.), to mind-manipulation ploys designed to help the ninja escape detection by clouding an enemy's mind.

The Art of Mysticism

Teaches students a myriad of concentration and mediation techniques designed to focus and strengthen the student's mind.

Advanced students are then taught techniques of mind manipulation (for example, evoking a foe's emotions, the use of subliminal suggestion, or hypnotism) designed to give ninja an edge against foes.

Attacking an enemy's mind is known as *saimen-jutsu* (storming the mind-gate.)

STORMING THE MIND-GATE

"Your greatest weapon is in your enemy's mind."

—Buddha

Ninja compared attacking another's mind to invading an enemy fortress, literally overwhelming their mental defenses (either through direct attack or through entering by stealth). Other accomplished mind masters have used the metaphor of "The City of Nine Gates" when speaking of the mental vulnerabilities of the body.

These "nine gates" are the nine bodily openings (eyes, ears, nose, mouth, urethra, and anus) through which we interact with the world (that is, how we receive information, express ourselves, experience pleasure, etc.).

A foe can thus be overcome by breaching one of these gates. For example, false gossip and propaganda attacks his ear gate; a sexual ploy can be used to attack his (urethra) sex gate.[2]

Ninja mind-manipulation experts employed a two-step strategy when attacking the mind of an enemy—first discerning and discovering, then distorting and destroying.

Step 1: Discerning an enemy's mind-set (overall attitude toward life, personal beliefs, etc.) and then discovering the inherent weaknesses they carry through the use of satsujin-jutsu allows us to prepare a mind strategy for invading a foe's mind castle.[3]

Step 2: After discerning an enemy's mind-set and discovering his inherent weaknesses, we then set about distorting our enemy's version of reality, figuratively and literally destroying his trust in the world and his confidence in himself.

Techniques designed to distort an enemy's view of the world around him (destroying his trust of others, undermining his self-confidence, etc.) are collectively known as *kiai-shin-jutsu* (shouting into another's mind).

Satsujin-Jutsu

In order to gain insight into another's mind (indeed, into our own minds) we must examine two factors:

First, we must explore the role nature (genetics, gender, the time and circumstance of our birth) plays in our overall make-up.

Second, we must examine the nurture factors in our lives (such as our birth order, our family relationships, and childhood trauma).

Master manipulators—from medieval ninja to modern cult leaders—are adroit at discerning and then distorting the part nature and nurture play in the overall make-up of their victims. Ninja sennin (mind masters) adopted mind-manipulation tactics from a variety of sources in addition to developing many unique mind-bending techniques of their own, each of which will be discussed at length later in this book.

However, at this point, a brief introduction to these tactics and techniques is in order:

Jujushin

A concept shinobi sennin adapted from Shingon Buddhism. Jujushin identifies "10 minds," 10 levels of understanding and functioning into which human beings can be categorized.

Discerning the jujushin level at which another person is operating at any given time gives us great insight into the mind and motivations of that person.

Ekkyo

These are divination methods that allow us to determine a victim's birth order and examine his interactions with others, especially close relatives. This allows us to attack an enemy by psychologically "cutting at the edges" of his world, that is, undermining his confidence by eroding his comfort zone.

Junishi-Do-Jutsu

Employs the ancient art of Chinese astrology to determine a person's overall temperament as well as his weakest time of the day, when he is most susceptible to physical attack and mental manipulation.

Having discerned an individual's overall modus operandi, having discovered his innate weaknesses, ninja sennin then deployed a variety of kiai-shinjutsu tactics and techniques designed to distort the victim's world and eventually destroy him.

Kiai-Shin-Jutsu

Kiai-shin-jutsu tactics and techniques directly attack the intended victim psychologically by "shouting" into his mind. Examples include:

In-Yo-Jutsu

These tactics are designed to unbalance an opponent, to sow doubt and distrust in his mind.

In-yo is the Japanese version of the Taoist concept of yin-yang (balance). The theory behind all in-yo tactics is to throw an opponent off balance by making him doubt himself and distrust others and to pull him from a sure-footed black-and-white way of looking at the world into a slippery-slope "gray area" where his trust in others and confidence in self begin to falter and flag.

Amettori-Jutsu (A Man of Straw)

Encompasses all tactics and techniques of deception. The name comes from the ploy of dressing up a scarecrow to make an enemy think it is a real sentry or soldier.

Gojo-Goyoku (Five Element Theory)

This was derived from the Chinese pseudo-science of wu-hsing, which teaches that all reality (including actions and attitudes) is composed of five basic forces: earth, air, fire, water, and void. In all things and all times, one of these elements is dominant. Each element has a corresponding element in opposition to it. When gojo-goyoku is specifically applied to emotions it is referred to as The Five Weaknesses or The Five Feelings.

Jomon-Jutsu

Consists of the use of special words and phrases designed to affect an individual's emotional stability, such as words evoking fear, lust, or patriotism.

Yugen-Shin-Jutsu (Mysterious Mind)

Uses various methods of hypnotism and subliminal suggestion to influence and control the minds of others.

Kyonin-No-Jutsu

Plays upon a person's superstitions, ranging from his belief in voodoo to believing that getting caught out in the rain causes illness.

ENDNOTES

1. Lung, Haha. *The Ancient Art of Strangulation*. Boulder, Colorado: Paladin Press, 1995.
2. Lung, Haha. *Assassin! Secrets of the Cult of Assassins*. Boulder, Colorado: Paladin Press, 1997.
3. If you think of yourself as a castle, the physical walls are your actual body and its innermost locked and guarded rooms are your mind. The gates, windows, and other openings allow others to spy on what is going on inside the castle and to enter that stronghold by stealth.

CHAPTER 2

UNDERSTANDING THE MIND

In his book *Street Ninja*, Dirk Skinner says that the more you know about how the human body is put together, the easier it is to take it apart.

The same holds true for the human mind.

The more we understand about the basic functioning of the human brain—how it "sees" the world around it, how it processes and stores information—the easier it is for us to guard the frontiers of our own minds while successfully mounting a campaign against the minds of our enemies.

HOW THE BRAIN SEES

The brain sees and then stores information, even the most complex of information, as simple picture-symbols. This holds true whether the brain is taking in information only through the eyes or through one of the other senses—hearing, smell, taste, or touch.

Try this experiment: Ask people to describe a spiral staircase. After searching for words to describe the staircase, observe how they inevitably draw pictures (symbols) of it in the air with their hands.

Now ask someone, "How many sides does a pyramid have?" Most people will say "three," correcting themselves only after you point out that a triangle has three sides, a three-dimensional pyramid, five. When you say "pyramid," your friend's brain hears "triangle" since the brain stores the memory of a pyramid (complex) behind the picture-symbol of a triangle (simple) in the "things that remind me of a triangle" file.

Consider this: "The United States of America" is a vast and complex notion. The concept of "U.S.A." incorporates such subconcepts as "liberty" and "the pursuit of happiness."

However, as complex as the actual physical entity of the U.S.A. is, all it takes is seeing a flag with stars and stripes, a scowling poster of Uncle Sam, or hearing a patriotic song on the radio for our brains to visualize the U.S.A. in all its glory.

Mind-masters, from Army recruiters to political spin-doctors, know the value of symbols that cause our minds to involuntarily form thoughts and images, symbols that trigger responses within us whether we want our minds to or not!

The Power of Visualization

Recent research conducted at Stanford University has verified what master mind manipulators have known for centuries: that mentally picturing doing an action in our minds causes our nervous system to react as if we were actually doing the action being imagined.

World-class athletes know the positive potential of such deliberate voluntary mental visualization training. In fact, an estimated 90 percent of sports figures practice some form of visualization. Shadow boxing employs visualization, as do ritual forms (kata) of martial arts.

On the more sinister side, unscrupulous mind-slayers know that involuntary visualization (e.g. reliving a catastrophic failure or traumatic assault over and over in the mind) serves only to perpetuate feelings of powerlessness and self-loathing.

Mind-slayers also know that simple words or even gestures can be used to purposely trigger involuntary images in another's mind. If you doubt this, flip a stranger "the bird" and see how quickly your single raised middle finger affects that stranger's mood. Why? Not because the digit itself is threatening, but because of the images the person forms in his mind when seeing that single finger.

Visualization works because, contrary to popular conception, our eyes are not cameras perfectly recording all the things that cross in front of our eyes. For example, when we look at an object, say a tree, we are not actually

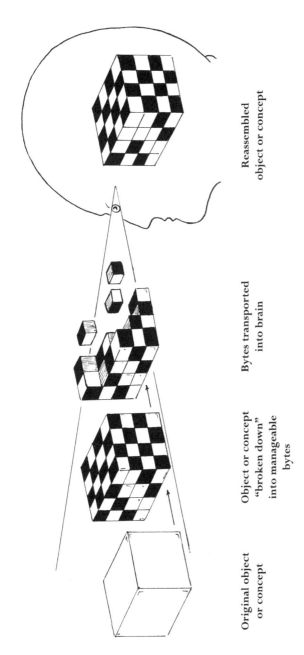

Reassembled
object or concept

Bytes transported
into brain

Object or concept
"broken down"
into manageable
bytes

Original object
or concept

seeing the tree perfectly reflected off some mirror in our brain. What we are seeing in our mind's eye is our brain's reassembled image of that tree.

Like *Star Trek*'s matter-transporter, our eyes "disassemble" the tree into manageable data-bytes (with information relating to the object's shape, size, color, etc.) and then "beam" (relay) that information in the form of electrical impulses into our brain, where an image of the tree is then reassembled.

Between breaking down the image into storable data bytes and reassembling those data bytes inside our heads, dozens of different filters affect how accurately we reassemble those data bytes.

These filters include:

- Physical defects in the structure of sense organs (such as colorblindness, poor hearing, or lack of taste buds);
- Defects in the brain itself (chemical imbalances, either natural or self-induced);
- Strong emotion and psychological concerns (e.g. fear, lust, or jealousy);
- Socially-imposed constraints and taboos (e.g. religious or racial prejudices).

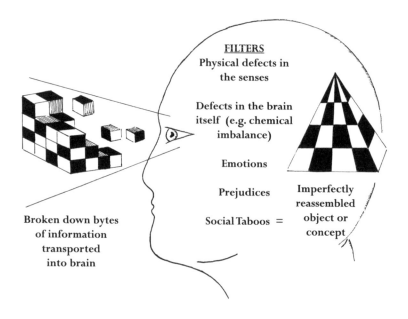

FILTERS
Physical defects in the senses

Defects in the brain itself (e.g. chemical imbalance)

Emotions

Prejudices

Social Taboos =

Imperfectly reassembled object or concept

Broken down bytes of information transported into brain

These filters affect how accurately an object (or an idea, for that matter) is reassembled inside our heads.

Killer Symbols

What teenager hasn't experienced an embarrassing wet dream? How is it that nightmares make our hearts beat faster? Why does merely thinking about asking the prom queen out on a date, asking the boss for a raise, or having to prepare for an important speech make us literally break out in a cold sweat?

It is because images from our internal world, our mind, can affect us externally by making us physically ill or ill at ease.

It is no secret that mental symbols can cause physical symptoms. For example, racist symbols may excite us, frighten us, or piss us off, causing us to tremble with rage. Likewise, patriotic symbols and team emblems stir our blood, causing our chests to swell with pride. In other words, a mental image or symbol can easily have physical consequence as significant as an actual physical experience.

Some experts maintain that mental images and symbols can affect our health because they communicate at a cellular level, directly influencing physical tissues and organs. This is one explanation for the documented power of voodoo-type curses to kill.

Medicine has documented the "placebo effect," in which patients given sugar pills they believe to be powerful narcotics relieve their own pain through the power of suggestion. Less well known is the "nocebo effect," in which patients, believing themselves to have terminal illnesses (or to be under curses) literally make themselves sick and die. In these instances, the patient's belief sets off a chain of mental images that culminate in the person physically making himself sick, perhaps even dying from fright.

Types of Symbols
". . . the mind of man contains only so many visions."
—Judith Hooper and Dick Teresi,
The Three-Pound Universe

How we respond to visualized symbols depends on the background and context in which the symbols appear and on the conditions under which we originally encountered their meaning.

There are three types of symbols: universal symbols, cultural-religious symbols, and symbols that have purely personal meaning. Adept mind-slayers learn to recognize and wield these different kinds of symbols in order to mentally and physically affect others' thoughts and actions.

Universal Symbols

Some symbols are universal and are found in all times, in all parts of the world. Psychology pioneer Carl Jung (1875-1961) called these universal symbols "archetypes."

For instance, in the 1920s, University of Chicago scientist Heinrich Kluver discovered four shapes that appeared in all mescaline hallucinations: the spiral, the tunnel (or funnel), the cobweb, and latticework (criss-crossing lines or honeycomb patterns). These "geometric constants" were subsequently verified in studies at UCLA in the 1970s.[1]

Such studies indicate that our brains are already hard-wired with certain universal symbols, the four discovered in these two studies, and perhaps others yet to be isolated.

Cultural-Religious Symbols

The meanings of other symbols are determined and defined by whatever particular culture or religion happens to be dominant at the time. Such symbols include religious figures and totems, tribal standards, and patriotic emblems.

Often in a culture, a particular religious or political figure will take on importance as a symbol to others, either positive or negative (e.g. Hitler, Gandhi, or Martin Luther King).

Personal Symbols

The third type of symbol is based on our individual experiences, pleasurable or traumatic.

Despite rationalizing, all of us respond to universal symbols and to cultural and political symbols. That's why Madison Avenue and other mind manipulation adepts are so good at making us buy things we don't need. In many instances however, personal interpretation of symbols seems able to override cultural, political, and even universal meanings of common symbols.

Take for example the near-universal depiction of the Father/Creator/God as a stern-faced old man with long white hair and a long white beard.

Compare Michelangelo's paintings of God with those of the Greco-Roman statues of Zeus and Jupiter, in turn, with those of Chinese "Immortals."

Although our logical adult brains might argue for God as a genderless, disembodied spirit, if we were raised under the scrutiny of a patriarchal culture or religion, this image of a wise and stern all-powerful father figure remains the symbol our brains "recognize" as God. This image in turn is compiled from, and associated with, images in our minds of omniscient wisdom and omnipotent authority.

While this Father/God symbol is near-universal, and is culturally and religiously reinforced, any such image must still be filtered through our personal symbol dictionary. For example, one individual dreaming of a wizened white-haired and bearded figure will feel blessed and awe-inspired by the image because it would represent his cultural/religious symbol of the benevolent patriarchal God. Conversely, a second dreamer, the victim of parental child abuse, may wake up screaming in terror at the image of an oppressive and abusive father figure dominating his dream.

The Power of Believing

The most important consideration determining how a person responds to any particular symbol is the amount of mental energy (focus) that person invests into that particular symbol, that is, how strongly he believes in that symbol.

The symbol of Uncle Sam (another stern white-bearded father figure, by the way) declaring "I want you!" is enough for some impressionable young people to pack up their ol' kit bags and head for the front. For others, the symbol of Uncle Sam does not evoke feelings of patriotism, pride, and unquestioning obedience. For these, hostile foreign nationals for example, the symbol of Uncle Sam may incite hatred and fear.

Belief is the most powerful of mental filters, determining whether information we reassemble inside our minds is reality, or merely a reflection of the way we'd like things to be.

It is both the actual and perceived power pumped into a symbol by a culture, clan, or by a traumatized individual himself that observant and opportunistic mind-slayers evoke and manipulate through use of that symbol.

Remember: It is belief that gives symbols their power. In other words, symbols are effective only when they stimulate a belief response in the subconscious.

Why do symbols work? Why are they such effective tools in the mind-slayer's bag of tricks?

One theory behind why symbols work so well, affecting us both mentally and physically, is that symbols bypass the critical and logical conscious part of our minds and talk directly to the nonjudgmental subconscious level of our minds.

It is at this subconscious level that the most adroit of mind-slayers ply their craft.

To recap:

The brain is not a camera. What the brain sees through the five senses is an all-too-often imperfect reconstruction.

Filters placed between an object (or information) perceived by the senses and the brain's reconstruction of that information influence and interfere with the brain's accurate reconstruction of that information.

These filters include such things as personal beliefs, strong emotion, past trauma, and cultural and religious prejudices.

By deliberately imposing such filters between the information perceived by the senses and its reconstruction in the brain, an accomplished mind-slayer can control how another person's mind sees.

MASTERING THE MIND (HARAGAGEI)

"Faced with a threatening challenge or confronted by
overwhelming odds, the untrained body panics. It is left to the
mind to realistically assess the situation and decide the proper
course of action: flight or fight, resistance or surrender, life or
death . . . A trained mind is an asset, a tool for survival."
—Dirk Skinner, *Street Ninja*

It is often said we humans use only 10 percent of our brains.

The truth is that we only consciously use a small percentage of our mental potential and, of the 10 percent or so we do consciously use, most of us don't use it effectively or efficiently.

Ninja students learned early on that survival and ultimate victory begin in the mind.

Medieval shinobi-ninja faced great physical and mental challenges, not the least of which was the stress of being under the constant threat of capture, torture, and death from overwhelming numbers of samurai invaders. Yet the shinobi-ninja overcame these challenges through the use of *seishin-shugi*, literally mind over matter.

Medieval ninja students began by learning the basic traditional and technical aspects of their chosen craft in order to survive. But, in order to master their craft, the ninja student had to pass beyond mere regurgitation of lessons, beyond mere repetition of technical physical skills.

Their first step was wiping their minds clear of psychological hindrances and mind filters (doubts, phobias, unresolved trauma, and prejudices), thus unleashing the endless potential and natural flow of the unclouded mind.

Likewise, we today need to discover our own filters, those mental programming glitches that prevent us from seeing the world clearly.

For survival, we must find these potentially fatal faults and mental fissures in our minds before our enemies do.

Seishinshugi: Mind over Matter

"All things are ready, if our minds be so."

—Shakespeare, *King Henry V*

Physical circumstances all too often overpower the mind. In the face of overwhelming force or impossible odds, confusion, doubts, and fear creep in and we falter. Doubt is the beginning of defeat.

Such doubts and fears amount to stains on the mirror of our minds, a mirror that should perfectly reflect the world around us but which, instead, reflects imperfectly because of these stains on its surface. Adroit mind-slayers deliberately insert confusion, doubt and fear into the minds of their foes, purposely staining the foe's mind-mirror in order to make that foe "see" an imperfect reflection of the world.

An imperfect reflection of the world around them causes people to act on incorrect information. Calculated on incorrect intelligence, an enterprise cannot but fail.

In order to remain in a constant state of readiness to do battle, be it physical battle or a no-less-lethal mental challenge, ninja cultivated *makoto*, the stainless mind. Makoto is a balanced state of mind allowing us to remain calm even in the most trying of circumstance.

The development of makoto consists of the active cultivation and practice of two skills: *haragei* (awareness), and *rinkioken* (adaptability).

Awareness

Medieval ninja practiced purposeful awareness of all five known senses (sight, hearing, taste, smell, and touch) as their first line of defense, as well as their first choice of offensive weapons when aggression was called for.

As children, we used all our senses to explore the world around us. As we grew older, however, our senses began to dull. For most adults, the use of the senses is not balanced—that is, we tend to favor one or more of our senses, while neglecting the others.

Unlike the average person, mind-slayers practice the full use of all five senses to the point that they notice every shift in weight; hear each slight hesitation of doubt in a person's voice; feel that slight tremble in another when shaking hands or brushing against him. The most accomplished of these mind-slayers can literally "smell" doubt and fear in another person. Used to their fullest, in concert with one another, the five known senses become greater than the sum of their parts, merging to create a sixth, extrasensory sense of awareness.

The effect of using their five trained senses together gave the impression to indolent and uninitiated outsiders that ninja mind-slayers possessed magic powers. Like modern mind manipulators, medieval ninja did nothing to discourage this belief.

When you practice being more attuned to the subtlety and nuance of your environment, and to the subconscious clues given off by others, it will appear to others that you possess magical extrasensory abilities though, in actuality, all you are doing is using to the fullest the same five senses we all possess but all too often take for granted.

And, if human beings do possess a long dormant and denied ESP—a sixth sense—what better way to develop it than by disciplining and making full use of our first five?

Adaptability

"Develop intuitive judgement and
understanding for everything . . .
Perceive those things which cannot be seen . . .
Pay attention even to trifles."

—Miyamoto Musashi

The ruling samurai of medieval Japan adhered to the rigid bushido code that dictated chivalry in civilian life and outlined restrictive rules when it came to personal combat between equals.

If medieval ninja had insisted on thinking and acting in the same manner as the rest of feudal Japanese society, the great ninja masters of Iga and Koga would not have survived to pass their secrets of success along to us.

The greatest of these ninja secrets of success was their rinkioken.

Ninja warriors were trained to think on their feet, to improvise rather than to adhere to a rigid game plan. Likewise, ninja sennin trained to see and think in unconventional, non-linear fashion in order to be able to enter at will a heightened state of calm awareness that allowed them to function at their peak physical and mental level. This level of awareness is known as entering the Zen-zone.

The Zen-zone is that level of functioning where stainless mental awareness (makoto) and physical awareness merge, allowing us to instantly and effortlessly adapt to rapidly shifting circumstance.

Master mind-slayers operate from this Zen-zone, remaining balanced and aware—guarding the walls of their own mind castles while constantly alert for any sign of weakness in a foe's mind defenses.

ENDNOTE

1.   Hooper, Judith and Dick Teresi. *The Three-Pound Universe*. New York: Macmillan, 1986.

CHAPTER 3

MASTERING OTHERS

"A keen insight into human psychology
and predictability has always proven
the ninja's greatest weapon. This
remains true today."
—Dirk Skinner, *Street Ninja*

INTRODUCTION: MIND CONTROL BY THE NUMBERS

After thousands of years of observing human behavior, accomplished mind-masters in India, Tibet, and China discovered and compiled shared patterns of behavior, catalogued innate relationships, and discerned what they believed to be "celestial correspondences" that influenced human actions and reactions.

Whatever the original benevolent intent for collecting and compiling this data, the end result—perhaps the inevitable result—was that this information fell into the hands of unscrupulous mind-slayers. They realized how easily such information, literally from inside a foe's mind, could be used to improve their own good fortune while bringing misfortune down upon the heads of their enemies.

It was also inevitable that these astute and potentially valuable observations from India, Tibet, China, and a dozen other ports of call all eventually found their way into the hands of adroit Japanese ninja mind-slayers.

From these ancient observations, ninja sennin gleaned those insights most likely to benefit their craft and clan. First they tested the validity and applicability of these ancient observations and then augmented them with tried-and-true observations from the pseudo-sciences and esotericism of various Japanese sources (indigenous Ainu shamanism, Yamabushi and Shinto mysticism, and Buddhist psychology).

Recall that Sun Tzu taught that "knowing your own mind is only half the battle." The other half is discerning the mind-set of others—their personal perceptions, motivations, and potential flaws (fears and prejudices) that correspond to or differ from your own.

It was vital for medieval ninja sennin to master the ability to read others, first in order to protect themselves, and then in order to benefit others in clan and community—just as it is vital that we today learn to do the same.

THE TWO WAYS

There are two basic approaches people take to life: *shodomon* and *jodomon*.

Shodomon, the way of the monkey, depends on *jiriki* (one's own strength).

Individuals with this approach to life are independent; journeying alone, finding their own way, keeping their own counsel, and binding their own wounds—both physically and psychically. On the one extreme, these kinds of people are rugged individualists. At the opposite extreme, they are stubborn isolationists and control freaks, unable to take another's counsel.

The second approach to life is jodomon, the way of the cat. Individuals who take this approach depend on *tariki* (another's power).

Tariki is represented by a baby kitten, carried lovingly in its mother's mouth. Jiriki, on the other hand, is symbolized by a baby monkey holding on for dear life while its mother swings from branch to branch.

Neither path is inherently better than the other. We all strive for independence and experience feelings of self-worth when we accomplish a goal through our own efforts. Just as often, however, are the times we need help to accomplish a difficult task. As with all things in life, rigidly clinging to the extreme of either of these positions creates conflict. Stubbornly refusing to ask for help when we need it is as dangerous as being chronically dependent on others for our safety, succor, and salvation.

Ideally, jiriki and tariki work hand-in-hand, with us seeking assistance and accepting guidance when we need it, while building on our own independence of being.

For safety's sake, we must determine our own personal outlook: jiriki, tariki or, ideally, the balance of the two.

By first clarifying your own approach to life, you will be able to better decipher the basic approach to life of others, especially your foes.

Bet your life, your foes are attempting to make the same assessment of you!

THE FIVE WEAKNESSES (GOJO-GOYOKU)

"When preparing to move against an enemy commander,
you must first scrutinize that commander's men in order to
discern whether those men are wise or stupid, adroit and eager
or hesitant. Only after determining the enemy's mind can you
prepare correct strategy."

—Tu Mu

As outlined in the section on kiai-shin-jutsu, much of the ninja mind-slayer's craft originated with the Chinese Taoist concept of wu-sing (The Five Elements, known in Japan as gojo-goyoku) which maintains that all reality is made up of five basic elements: earth (chi), air (fu), fire (la), water (sui), and void (ku).

Constantly interacting, these elements either strengthen or diminish one another.

Over the centuries, the interactions of these five elements have been extensively cataloged and found to correspond to all aspects of life:

FIVE ELEMENTS CORRESPONDENCE

Interaction	Result	Technique/Example
Wood creates Fire	Burning	Anger creates joy (excitement, "adrenaline junkies").
Fire creates Earth	Ash	Joy (active) creates sympathy (passive).
Earth creates Metal	Ore	Sympathy creates sloth (Use altruism and trap him with sympathy ploys).
Metal creates Water	Condensation, Smelting	Sloth creates fear. (Turn fear and powerlessness into defeatism).
Water creates Wood	Growth, Irrigation	Fear creates anger. (Plant paranoia and cultivate his cowardice.)

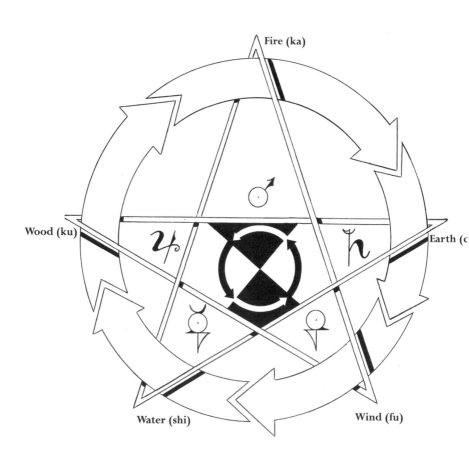

Wood overcomes Water	Damming	Anger defeats fear. (Frustrate his plans and then turn his frustration to your agenda).
Water overcomes Fire	Extinguishing	Fear snuffs out joy. (Paranoia poisons pleasure.)
Fire overcomes Metal	Melting	Joy defeats sloth. (Upset his routine with offers "too good to be true.")
Metal overcomes Wood	Chopping	Sloth defeats anger. (Laziness and procrastination upset his timetable.)
Wood overcomes Earth	Growth of roots	Anger defeats sympathy. (Convince him "The Cause" has turned its back on him.)

When applied by ninja sennin to human emotions and attitudes for insight into the mind, the five elements are gojo-goyoku, (The Five Weaknesses).

Gojo-Goyoku

In all people at all times, one of five distinct feelings dominates: fear (*kyosha*), lust (*kisha*), anger (*dosha*), greed (*rakusha*), or sympathy (*aisha*). A mnemonic aid for helping remembering these five feelings is "FLAGS," as in warning flags.

During the course of an average day, all of these five feelings can manifest.

Like the wu-hsing elements that rule over them, these emotions are not static, but constantly in flux, with one feeling augmenting or canceling out another. But one of these feelings is always dominant in each of us. This dominant feeling produces our personality and our overall attitude toward the world.

Learning to discern a person's overall personality element allows mind-slayers to adroitly introduce and influence elements of mood and personality in order to manipulate a foe's attitude and outlook at any given time.

The Five Weaknesses were first employed by moshuh nanren, and were committed to writing by such master strategists as Sun Tzu and Tu Mu.

Subsequently, down through the centuries, military strategists, martial artists, and mind-slayers have all used The Five Weaknesses to overcome foes.

Sun Tzu isolated the five fatal flaws for a general 2,500 years ago. They are: arrogance, fear, being quick to anger; concern over losing face and honor; and being overly sympathetic (and thus hesitant).

Strategist Tu Mu (803-852 CE) likewise used his knowledge of The Five Feelings when giving advice on how to recruit spies from enemy territory. He taught how to uncover traitors bitter at having been passed over for promotion, those ruled by greed who could be bribed, opportunists willing to take advantage of troubled times, and deceitful men without honor.

Modern Application of Gojo-Goyoku

In his book *Street Ninja*, Dirk Skinner explains modern applications of gojo-goyoku by urban survivalists seeking to add another weapon to their defensive arsenal, as well as by unsavory characters seeking to manipulate others.

For example, modern-day criminals use female assistants to distract their victims in much the same way female ninja first distracted and then dispatched foes by appealing to their lust. Likewise, modern con men seek out that little bit of greed in us all, and/or play on overly sympathetic victims.

On the flip-side, Skinner shows how a robbery victim can fake a seizure and cause a mugger who's only after money to flee in fear as he's convinced his intended victim is having a heart attack, thus turning the attempted robbery into a homicide! Skinner also shows how anger ploys can be used in self-defense to incite an attacker into making mistakes—often fatal ones.

Despite their English translations, none of the gojo-goyoku are in and of themselves negative. Each has its positive aspect as well as its negative side. For example, dosha (anger) is negative when vented indiscriminately. However, righteous anger—anger expressed over an injustice—is "good" anger.

With insight worthy of a modern psychologist, Tu Mu relates how, after seizing a large cache of booty, the troops of General Tu Hsing were weakened by greed and lost their desire to fight. To remedy this, Tu Hsing secretly sent agents to burn his own men's barracks and the treasure they'd stored there. The wily general then blamed the fire on enemy spies, thus using anger to defeat greed, and once more incite his men against their foe.

It is important to keep in mind that these Five Feelings can appear in either benevolent or malevolent garb. For example, kisha can manifest as negative obsessive lust or as positive passion. Likewise, fear can paralyze us or can galvanize us to flight or fight.

THE FIVE WEAKNESSES

Weakness:	Anger	Lust	Sympathy	Greed	Fear
Element:	Void/Wood	Fire	Earth	Wind/Metal	Water
Japanese Name:	Ku	Ka	Chi	Fu	Sui
Positive Emotion	Justice	Joy, Love	Compassion	Focus	Vigilance
Negative Emotion	Rage, violence	Lust, frustration	Pity, helplessness	Sloth, ruthlessness	Cowardice, phobias
Your Attack Strategy	Crush: Press, overpower coup de grace	Pound: Repeated blows 1-2 punch	Cross: Bypass, "Cutting at The Edges"	Split: Alienate him from his supporters	Drill: Worm your way into confidence, plant seeds of doubt.
Your Defense Strategy	Retreat: Fall back to Plan "B"	Shift Right: Right = Imagination. Excite his imagination.	Even: Zen-face, show nothing	Advance: Press advantage, pressure ploys	Shift Left: Left = Memory. Invoke the past.
Dominant Sense	Vision	Speech	Taste	Smell	Touch
Focus	Communication	Intellect	Physical body	Wisdom	Emotions
Attitude	Creativity	Enthusiasm	Stability	Benevolent	Adaptability

Instead of merely targeting a victim's mind with a single emotional strike, accomplished mind-slayers often deliver a "one-two punch," attacking an enemy's mind with a combination of emotions, thus seeding confusion.

For example, Chinese strategist Chen Hao knew how to use the Five Weaknesses, attacking an enemy with greed (rakusha) while throwing in a healthy dose of lust (kisha) to further unnerve the foe:

"Entice an enemy with young boys and maidens to distract him,
offer jade and fine silk to draw out his greed," he advised.

Likewise, Sung Dynasty strategist Chang Yu pointed out how emotional shortcomings could bring down an enemy:

"To control a foe, first anger him, then confuse him,
then teach him fear without rest. Thus he loses his will to fight,
thus he loses his ability to plan."

Predatory mind-slayers master the intricacies of the gojo-goyoku in order to control others. Thus, we must put effort into the study of The Five Weaknesses if only for self-defense.

Rakusha (Greed) Ploys

"See, sons, what things you are! How quickly nature falls
into revolt when gold becomes her object!"
—Shakespeare, *King Henry IV*

Sun Tzu says the sure way to control an enemy is by appealing to his greedy nature; entice him with something he is certain to want (such as an easy victory) and with promises of easy gain.

Likewise, Tu Mu points out how potential traitors can be swayed by appeals to their greed and licentiousness.

Confidence men count on their victims not reporting having been swindled. First, the victim doesn't want to look as foolish as he feels for having been duped. Second, he doesn't want to look greedy, since greed—the desire for the fast buck—is what often entices them into the con man's trap in the first place.

Like all the Five Weaknesses, greed can be deadly.

A classic wartime ploy is to scatter valuable—but booby-trapped—souvenirs, such as swords or other weapons, in the path of advancing enemy troops.

Chinese astrology warns that people born under the sign of the Snake never let an opportunity slip, and are thus prime candidates for any too-good-to-be-true offer mind-slayers wave in front of their faces.

For our own self-defense, when tempted by the lure of easy gain we would do well to remember the ancient Chinese adage:

"Under fragrant bait there is certain to be found a hooked fish."

Dosha (Anger) Ploys
"Never anger made good guard for itself."
—Shakespeare, *Anthony and Cleopatra*

Tu Mu illustrates the cost of uncontrolled anger with the story of the general who, rather than sending his enemy counterpart the traditional exchange of wine between equals, instead sent the rival general a pot of urine. In his rage, the offended general imprudently ordered his men to attack a heavily-defended stronghold, with predictably disastrous results.

Whether in a major battlefield engagement, in one-on-one martial arts combat, or when engaged in high-stakes negotiations, seeding anger in a foe's mind clouds his reason, opening the way to his defeat.

Thus, samurai warrior Kojiro Okinaga, one of Miyamoto Musashi's early teachers, instructed the young Musashi:

"Goad your foe into attacking before he is ready, and you will always gain the advantage over him."

Musashi never forgot this instruction, using the strategy to his advantage on many occasions. Mind-slayers know that a single word spoken at the right time or a single gesture can incite an otherwise calm and calculating foe into making a reckless mistake.

Kyosha (Fear) Ploys
"Of all base passions, fear is the most accurs'd."
—Shakespeare, *King Henry VI*

When we think of using fear against our enemies, we inevitably think of making an enemy fear us. After all, as the old adage says:

"Reputation often spills less blood."

In 518 BCE when the armies of Wu and Ch'u met, the commander of the Wu, realizing that the Ch'u forces were all too eager for battle, ordered 3,000 condemned men brought from Wu prisons. Since they were already condemned to death, the commander of the Wu promised these men that their families would be well cared for after their deaths provided they performed one final task for the Wu commander.

When all 3,000 agreed, the Wu commander had the prisoners dressed in Wu uniforms and placed in front of his troops, directly across the battlefield and in full view of the eager Ch'u troops. The Wu commander then sent a message to the Ch'u telling them to watch closely as the Wu commander demonstrated the loyalty and determination of his troops.

At a prearranged signal, all 3,000 condemned men cut their own throats! Believing these to be real Wu troops, Ch'u forces fled in terror.

Sinan, leader of the infamous Syrian hashishins (assassins) used a similar ploy, ordering his fanatical warriors to commit suicide in full view of visiting dignitaries in order to intimidate those guests into paying tribute.[1]

Ninja and other killer cadres deliberately cultivated an atmosphere of fear around themselves, realizing that the superstition and fear in which their enemies held them protected them as well as (if not better than) any armor.

A second way to use fear is to make enemies think we fear them. Says Sun Tzu:

"Pretend inferiority and encourage an enemy's arrogance."

According to Tu Mu, one can only feign weakness and fear effectively by being extremely strong.

The best illustration of this is the true story of "The 47 Ronin."

In 1701, Lord Kira, the shogun's master of ceremonies, knowing his long-time enemy Daimyo Asano to be a man easily brought to anger, deliberately provoked Lord Asano into drawing his sword on the shogun's grounds—a capital offense. For this breach of etiquette, Lord Asano was ordered to commit *seppuku* (ritual suicide).

At the time, Lord Asano had 47 samurai retainers. As was the custom of the time, many thought that at least some of Lord Asano's 47 knights would commit *hari-kiri* and follow their master into the void. At the very least, to save "face" and guard their honor, many believed the 47 should have launched a suicidal attack against the vastly superior number of samurai guarding Lord Kira. But it appeared their fear of dying prevented any of the 47 from doing so.

For two years thereafter, wherever one these 47 *ronin* (masterless samurai) went in Japan, they were reviled as the scum of the earth. Fathers pointed the 47 out to their sons as examples of how not to be, of what happens when samurai lose their honor.

Then, on the second anniversary of their master's death, all 47 ronin secretly gathered outside Lord Kira's residence and breached its walls. Caught by surprise, Lord Kira's samurai fell beneath the blades of the ronin. The following morning, the ronin placed Lord Kira's head on Lord Asano's grave and then, one by one, all 47 committed hari-kiri, finally joining their lord in the void.

Those 730 days during which the 47 ronin had to pretend to be fearful of death, fearful of the hated Lord Kira, must have been the hardest of their lives. Yet their strategy succeeded.

It is classic guerilla strategy for a small force to take potshots at a larger enemy force and then flee, drawing the pursuing enemy into an ambush. Custer learned this the hard way, as did U.S. troops in Vietnam.

Aisha (Sympathy) Ploys
"Of pity is the virtue of law,
And none but tyrants use it cruelly."
—Shakespeare, *Timon of Athens*

You're standing at a bus stop and the person next to you drops an object. Being the kindhearted person you are, you instinctively reach down to pick up the object for them and receive a knee to the face for your trouble. The purposely butter-fingered mugger takes your wallet and flees.

You have just fallen victim to a sympathy ploy.

Criminals and con men are adept at using sympathy ploys (a.k.a. "Good Samaritan traps") to cause us to stop to help that "stranded motorist" along that deserted stretch of road, or cause us to open our doors to a lost traveler just needing to use the phone.

Sometimes the cost of falling for a sympathy ploy is high. For example, serial killer Ted Bundy often wore a fake cast on his arm in order to elicit the sympathy of women he'd targeted.

Another sympathy shortcoming, this one rooted in fear, is fear of hurting others. Accomplished word-wizards have a variety of ploys they use to make us hold our tongues in order to avoid offending another person—our silence giving our implicit approval.

Having a fear of casualties is a fatal flaw in a general, according to Sun Tzu.

Tu Mu also warns that too much sympathy for troops leads to short-sightedness in a commander, who is then unable to give up a temporary advantage (in numbers) in order to achieve ultimate victory. This is, as Chinese strategists put it, "To let go of this in order to seize hold of that."

Both lust and greed can lead to recklessness. Yet no less fatal is allowing excessive concern or misplaced sympathy to cause us to hesitate. To hesitate (out of misplaced sympathy) to deliver the coup de grace once a rabid dog has been put down can prove costly, whether one is dealing with a mugger or Sadaam Hussein.

Kisha (Lust) Ploys
"And careless lust stirs up a desperate courage."
—Shakespeare, *Venus and Adonis*

Even the Bible is full of stories where lust played a deadly or near-deadly role:

- Joseph was cast into prison after spurning the lust of the wife of his Egyptian master.
- When lust clouded his better judgement, Samson got screwed by Delilah.
- King David's lust caused him to arrange the death of Uriah, so he could seize the dead man's wife. (David's plot qualifies as a cutting-at-the-edges ploy.)

Lust is simply greed with genitals attached. It's much akin to greed, with blind ambition lurking somewhere between the two.

From frustrated lust is born jealousy. *Othello* testifies to how easily lust masquerading as jealousy can be manipulated by an unscrupulous mind-slayer.

Realizing that all of us are susceptible to these Five Weaknesses, medieval ninja sennin learned to guard their own mind castles from such strategies, bringing their own emotions under control before they fell under the control of wily foes.

It is vital we exorcise our own emotional demons—learning which of the Five Feelings dominate our overall personalities, and which manifest in response to specific stimuli that our enemies are all too eager to supply!

Mindfulness of our own feelings and a realistic assessment of our own emotional strengths and weaknesses help us better guard ourselves against mental frustration welling up within, and from arrows of manipulation aimed at us from without by barbarians attempting to storm our mind castle.

THE EIGHT RELATIONSHIPS

"You can pick your friends, you can't pick your relatives."
—Anonymous

There is no avoiding the fact that others influence us—either positively or negatively. Nowhere is this truer than when it comes to close relatives.

In the West, breaking free from their parents' control, striking out on their own, and gaining independence is the goal of all young people. Conversely, in the East, traditionally the success or shame of any single family member reflects on the family as a whole. Thus, the overall function—or dysfunction—of an individual is intimately tied to his position in, and interactions with, the family.

Ancient Eastern masters—the first psychologists and sociologists—studied how an individual's role within the family, his birth order and his interactions with others, affected that person's overall approach to life.

By observing interactions between immediate family members, ancient masters discovered that the attitude individuals used inside the family were the same as those individuals used when dealing with people outside the immediate family.

For example, we tend to offer authority figures the same respect and deference we do our father. Likewise, a man's respect for his mother, sisters, and wife is reflected in his overall attitude toward females outside the immediate family. Thus, when developing strategies to overshadow another's mind, adroit mind-slayers look not only at the targeted individual, but also at the people (family, friends, etc.) comprising that target's support network.

The targeted individual and those offering him shelter and succor can be compared to links in a chain. If that chain is rattled or broken anywhere along its length, the main person targeted cannot help but be affected.

Mind-slayers begin by looking at immediate family, then surrogate family (i.e. boss = father, etc.), before then factoring in such things as birth order and even their target's astrological sign.

The Pakua

Five thousand years ago, while examining markings on tortoise shells, Chinese master Fu Hei discovered the Taoist science of *pakua* (pronounced "bok-wall"), the eight trigrams.

Pakua are eight symbols consisting of three lines each. Each symbol represents one of eight basic relationships and interactions of life. Pakua comes from the Taoist concept of yin-yang (representing Mother-Father). It is then sub-divided into six further expressions, three masculine, three feminine.

Though named for immediate family, the pakua is not limited only to interactions between immediate family. Pakua also reflects how we interact with other people, depending on how we see them (i.e. as surrogate family members).

Fu Hei maintained that these eight basic relationships could also be used to explain all human relationships.

Further study by Fu Hei revealed numerous other correspondences between pakua, human attitudes and health, and the universal qualities of the cosmos. Modern interpreters of pakua have used these eight relationships to devise strategies for business and even for negotiations between nations.

Note: Around 1100 BCE, Fu Hei's original eight trigrams were expanded to 64 hexagrams by Kin Wen (whose son founded the Chou Dynasty). These 64 hexagrams formed the basis of the I-Ching method of Taoist divination, another method favored by Eastern mind-slayers for insight into the minds of others.

Birth Order

It took another 5,000 years for modern Western sociologists to determine that Fu Hei was on to something, that our birth order indeed affects both our overall attitude and the path we take in life. In Western psychology, Alfred Adler (1870-1937) is credited with pioneering the idea that a person's place in family helps determine his or her personality.

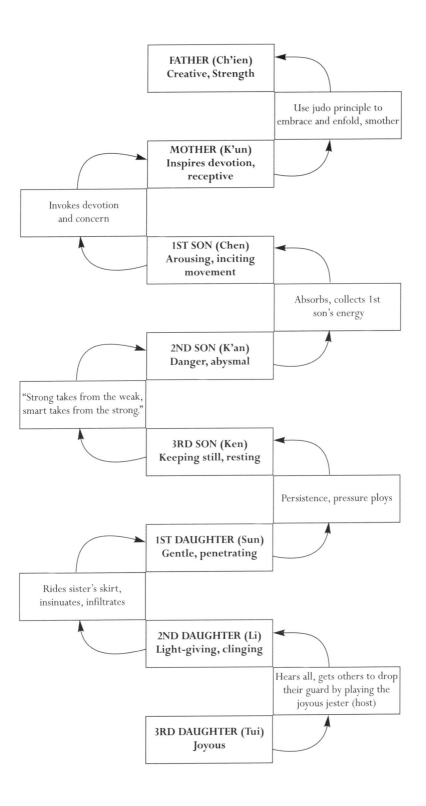

Proponents have used birth order to determine parenting styles and compatibility of potential mates. Madison Avenue opinion shapers factor in birth order when designing advertising campaigns.

Mind-slayers also study birth order. For example, they know that later-born children develop an array of strategies to distinguish themselves from earlier-born siblings. They therefore tend to be more creative and rebellious. They are also sympathetic to the underdogs, which makes them more vulnerable to sympathy ploys.

Knowing a person's birth order, mind-slayers gain invaluable insight into how to approach that person. An overview:

First-Borns

First-borns thrive on responsibility and are thus prone to be over-achievers. As a result, first-born children are often leaders, chieftains, entrepreneurs, explorers, and astronauts (six of the first seven U.S. astronauts who flew space missions were either first-born or only children).

Yet just as many first-borns are daring bank robbers and suave confidence men. The early bird gets the worm, thus first-borns are usually better educated.

First-borns are generally reliable, conscientious, and secure in positions of authority. They tend to stick close to their parents' values and be conservative. Taken to extremes, first-borns can be obsessive authoritarian perfectionists who are never satisfied, neither with themselves nor with others who fail to live up to the impossible standards first-borns all too often set.

Notable first-borns include writer Ayn Rand, Chinese leader Mao Tse Tung, and American presidents George Washington and Bill Clinton.

Middle-Borns

Middle-borns learn to be creative in order to develop the strategies and skills necessary to distinguish themselves from earlier and later siblings.

Trapped in the middle, these individuals are born negotiators (Martin Luther King and George Bush), wheeler-dealers (Donald Trump and Castro), and adroit power-brokers (Nixon).

Last-Borns

Last-born children are the pampered "babies" of the family and thus tend to be spoiled.

Many last-borns are easygoing, popular, and natural comedians (Eddie Murphy, John Candy, George Carlin, Billy Crystal, and Goldie Hawn).

However, even successful last-borns can nonetheless remain insecure and vulnerable. As a result, they are prone to risk-taking (consider Ben Franklin's electric kite, Gandhi's passive resistance, and Ronald Reagan's dangerous rhetoric and saber-rattling).

Mind-slayers know that last-born individuals are often susceptible to risky offers others might let pass.

Only Children

Only children have many of the characteristics of first-borns.

While reliable, conscientious, well organized, serious, and scholarly, they too can be overly critical perfectionists. Trying to imitate their parent's high standards, only children often secretly feel inferior and are plagued by feelings of inadequacy.

Notable only children include Leonardo da Vinci, FDR, Nancy Reagan, Ted Koppel, Lucille Ball, Joe Montana, and Elvis Presley (whose twin died at birth).

Six Degrees of Separation

In an experiment done in 1967, controversial psychology researcher Stanley Milgram established the principle of "six degrees of separation," showing that every person on Earth is connected to every other person on Earth within six people.

Six degrees of separation works like this: You may not personally have ever met the president of the United States. However, your high school sweetheart went on to marry a lawyer whose boss plays golf with the vice-president, who we assume has the president's ear. Thus, you are connected to the president within four people.

Theoretically, a rumor slipped into your ex-sweetheart's ear can conceivably find its way to the president. Since the president has, in turn, met with many world leaders, you are "connected" to most of the leaders of the world within five people.

Closer to home, six degrees connections can allow a mind-slayer to manipulate a foe's attitude and actions from afar, by seeding rumors, doubts, and misinformation to people in a direct line to the targeted foe.

Once the dominoes are all in a line, when one falls, they all fall. While your foe would never think of accepting a piece of information from you, he will readily listen to that same information when told to him by a close friend or relative.

A rumor repeated often enough becomes the truth. How more quickly when we are told the rumor by a source we trust? This six-degrees tactic falls under the strategy known as cutting at the edges.

Cutting at the Edges

In *A Book of Five Rings* (1643), Miyamoto Musashi advises that when an opponent cannot be overcome directly, one must attack with obliquity, drawing off his energies, weakening his center in preparation for a more direct final and fatal assault. Says Musashi:

> "If his corners are overthrown, the spirit of his whole
> body will be overthrown."

Thus, a mind-slayer planning to move against a foe will first determine what stress that foe is under (e.g. personal doubts, family, relationship or business problems) and then exacerbate those stressors. Where such stress does not already exist, the mind-slayer creates it.

Rather than attack an enemy directly, mind-slayers are adept at creating stressful "peripheral events" in a foe's life designed to divide that foe's energies and undermine his focus, making the foe more vulnerable to attack. Consider: What might be the effect on an athlete if his father was the victim of a coma-inducing mugging right before an important play-off game? Would concern destroy his concentration, or would it galvanize him to "Win one for the Gipper"? How might a targeted executive fare at a major business presentation if his indispensable secretary failed to show up for work that day because her son had been arrested for drug possession the day before?

The Kama Sutra recognized how important the people surrounding us are—whether we are plotting to secure a bride or to usurp a throne. The book describes in detail how to use a wife to get at her husband, to either sway his opinion or to set him up to be killed.

Other timely cutting-at-the-edges advice from *The Kama Sutra* includes:

- Frequent the same establishments and use the same businesses of the family you are trying to ingratiate yourself with.
- Become friends with the brother of the girl you are trying to seduce.
- Encourage one enemy to commit adultery with another enemy's wife. Once discovered, one enemy will kill the other. (This is known as "get a dog to eat a dog," or "the enemy of my enemy is my friend.")
- Show kindness to any trusted friend to whom the targeted girl gives her secret trust. A modern-day scenario of this ploy might involve getting to the president of the United States by getting a trusted friend of the president's former girlfriend to wear a wire. (Nah, never happen!)

THE NINE ROLES ("ALL THE WORLD'S A STAGE . . .")

Recall from our discussion of pakua that our place in the family and how we relate to family members helps determine how we look at the world and how we deal with people outside our immediate family circles.

In addition to pakua positions, there are five relationship pairings we use in dealing with other people: father-to-son, husband-to-wife, older sibling-to-younger, master-to-disciple, and friend-to-friend.

These five pairings in turn create nine basic roles we assume when dealing with others: father (i.e. authority), son, husband, wife, older sibling, younger sibling, master/teacher, disciple/servant, and friend.

With the exception of a true friend-to-friend relationship (a balanced relationship), in any of these pairings we can play either role. For example, in an interaction where one person has clear authority over another, we can assume the role of either the authority figure "father" or the respectful and obedient "son." This basic interpersonal dynamic can be further broken down into sub-roles and sub-scripts (e.g. obedient son versus obstinate son, a benevolent father versus a totalitarian one).

Mind-slayers learn to recognize these roles in others and become adept at adopting these roles when necessary, always taking on the role that will allow them to best control and manipulate the situation. Thus, mind-slayers do not always assume the dominant (father) role in an interaction. For the out-gunned guerilla, there are times to pretend fear and play a subservient role in order to get his foe to drop his guard, and/or in order to draw his enemy into an ambush.

The mind-slayer's battlefield is the mind, no less deadly. Master mind-slayers deliberately choose words and symbols that allow them and their agent-propagandists to assume the roles of our friends, surrogate parents, teachers, historical and mythical heroes, respected religious figures, even gods—all trusted figures to our subconscious, no matter how suspicious our conscious remains!

This explains the use and appeal of such titles as Holy Father, calls to fight and die for the motherland, and why your Uncle Sam wants you!

The more we understand about the use of symbols and universal archetypes and how easily such symbols can be used to manipulate us —whether by Madison Avenue or Charlie Manson—the better for our overall self-defense, both physical and mental.

On the offense side, the more we know about the wielding of such symbols, the easier it will be for us to tug at the heartstrings of our enemies—and eventually wrap those heartstrings tightly around their necks!

THE 12 BEASTS

On the eve of a great battle, Miyamoto Musashi noticed that the daimyo (samurai lord) with whom he had taken service seemed unable to focus on the impending battle. Asked what was the matter, the daimyo told Musashi that an astrologer had predicted that he, the daimyo, would soon die.

Shocked by this, Musashi called for the astrologer in the daimyo's presence. When the astrologer presented himself, Musashi questioned the wizard.

"Where do you get this information that our lord will soon die?" Musashi asked.

"All is written in the stars," the astrologer answered cryptically.

"And when do the stars say you will die?" Musashi asked.

"The stars predict that I will live a long life, find fame and fortune, and have many offspring!" the wizard proclaimed confidently.

At this point, Musashi's sword separated the wizard's head from his shoulders.

Placing the head of the astrologer at the feet of the shocked daimyo, Musashi explained to the samurai lord: "If a man is unable to predict his own fate, what hope has he of predicting the fate of others?" (Postscript: the decapitated astrologer was later discovered to have been a spy planted in the daimyo's court to unnerve him.)

Whether we think astrology is valid or not matters only so far as it can work to our advantage—either to give us insight into ourselves, or insight into our enemy's way of thinking. Knowing that foes believed in astrology armed medieval ninja sennin with yet one more defensive/offensive weapon.

In more modern times, during World War II, British intelligence maintained an Occult Bureau with astrologers on staff, all because it was well known that Hitler and many other Nazi big-wigs believed in astrology. This Occult Bureau used astrologers to figure out what Hitler's astrologers were telling him on any given day, hence, how the dictator might be expected to act.

Chinese Astrology

Astrology has always been popular throughout the East. Astrologers were as valued in ancient Imperial China as in the courts of ancient Babylon, Egypt, and among ancient Druids and Incas.

Astrology was practiced in China from ancient times, and was still thriving in the 13th century when Marco Polo recorded that the city of Kanbalu had more than 5,000 astrologers under the protection and patronage of the Emperor. These wizards used a variety of fortune-telling methods to forecast weather and the prophesy floods, epidemics, war, and conspiracy. But by far the most popular was their casting of horoscopes.

Eastern astrology is based on the longest chronological record in history, the Chinese Lunar calendar. A cycle of this calendar is completed every 60 years, and is further broken down into five subcycles of 12 years each. Our current 60-year cycle began in 1984.

According to legend, the Emperor of Heaven (later identified with Buddha) sent invitations out to all animals inviting them to a great feast, but only 12 beasts answered the summons. These 12 beasts were rewarded by the Emperor, who named each year of the 12-year cycle after one of them: Rat, Ox, Tiger, Rabbit, Dragon, Snake, Horse, Sheep, Monkey, Cock, Dog, and Pig.

Over centuries of observation, Chinese astrologers recorded the tendencies of persons born in each year and discovered that the animal ruling the year we are born has a profound influence on our personality and potentiality. Says the ancient Chinese adage: "This is the animal which hides in your heart."

Believers insist that understanding your "birth beast" gives you insight into yourself and helps you avoid disaster by advising you when best to act, and when to refrain from acting.

So popular did Chinese astrology become that, over the centuries, it spread throughout the Far East, including Japan. Today, at sunset on the streets of Tokyo, sidewalk fortune-tellers known as *ekisha* set up booths. Dressed in black kimonos, these mysterious individuals use astrology, palmistry, and consult the I Ching to tell the fates of passers-by. Many ekisha trace themselves and their arcane craft back to medieval ninja sennin mind-masters.

Besieged and bedeviled at every turn, any advantage the shinobi ninja could get over their foes was highly prized. Thus, any added insight ninja sennin could get into a foe's personality—both strengths and weaknesses— aided the ninja's survival of self and clan.

When Chinese astrology was first introduced to Japan, shinobi immediately recognized it as a valuable tool and weapon. From the ninja sennin's mastery of Chinese astrology came the ninja art of junishi-do-justu, cataloguing valuable clues for undermining the seemingly impenetrable walls of a foe's mind castle.

Killer Astrology (Junishi-Do-Jutsu)

For mind-slayers, a foe's birth year reveals valuable information about that foe's personality, insights that can be used when plotting strategy (for example inherent strengths and weaknesses and indications of when a foe is the weakest and thus most vulnerable to attack).

Study of junishi-do-jutsu also warns mind-slayers of their own inherent times of weakness, when they should refrain from action, times when a foe—who also studies junishi-do-jutsu—might target them!

THE 12 BEASTS

Beast	Strength	Strongest Time	Weakest Time	Enemy	Weakness to Exploit
Rat	Smart, quick-witted	11 P.M. to 1 A.M.	5 P.M. to 7 P.M.	Cock	Play to Rat's vanity. Trap him with a mystery. Rat is a social animal— draw him in by making him your guest of honor.
Ox	Big-hearted, long-suffering	1 A.M. to 3 A.M.	7 P.M. to 9 P.M.	Dog	Trap Ox with sympathy ploys. Ox tries to live up to the expectations of others. Offer to show him how to do this.
Tiger	Keeps promises	3 A.M. to 5 A.M.	9 P.M. to 11 P.M.	Pig	Suspicious by nature, feed his paranoia.
Rabbit	Clever, talented	5 A.M. to 7 A.M.	11 P.M. to 1 A.M.	Rat	Self-indulgent. Trap him by praising his talent. Play to his "lucky streak."
Dragon	Energetic, direct	7 A.M. to 9 A.M.	1 A.M. to 3 A.M.	Ox	Use the judo principle. Support his plans until he overloads, then turn his energy against him.
Snake	Quick to seize an opportunity	9 A.M. to 11 A.M.	3 A.M. to 5 A.M.	Tiger	Trap Snake with an offer he can't refuse, an opportunity "too good to be true."

Beast	Strength	Strongest Time	Weakest Time	Enemy	Weakness to Exploit
Horse	Hardworking	11 A.M. to 1 P.M.	5 A.M. to 7 A.M.	Rabbit	A workaholic, quick to anger. Help him work himself to death.
Sheep	Respectful, peaceful	1 P.M. to 3 P.M.	7 A.M. to 9 A.M.	Dragon	A homebody. Panics when home life is threatened. Use cutting-at-the-edges ploy.
Monkey	Energetic, full of plans. An inventor	3 P.M. to 5 P.M.	9 A.M. to 11 A.M.	Snake	Trap Monkey by making all his schemes and dreams seem possible. Has a short attention span.
Cock	Punctual	5 P.M. to 7 P.M.	11 A.M. to 1 P.M.	Horse	Predictable, his routine can be the death of him. Never admits he's wrong, tries to cover up mistakes, which leaves him open to blackmail.
Dog	Loyal, keeps secrets well	7 P.M. to 9 P.M.	1 P.M. to 3 P.M.	Sheep	Bureaucrat. Easily led. Doesn't like phonies. Make him think he's been betrayed.
Pig	Home-loving. Likes comfort, has faith in others	9 P.M. to 11 P.M.	3 P.M. to 5 P.M.	Monkey	Prone to laziness. Entice Pig with promises of increased comfort. Undermine his faith in those around him by cutting at the edges.

JUNISHI-DO-JUTSU BIRTH DATES

Rat	1936	1948	1960	1972	1984	1996	2008
Ox	1937	1949	1961	1973	1985	1997	2009
Tiger	1938	1950	1962	1974	1986	1998	2010
Rabbit	1939	1951	1963	1975	1987	1999	2011
Dragon	1940	1952	1964	1976	1988	2000	2012
Snake	1941	1953	1965	1977	1989	2001	2013
Horse	1942	1954	1966	1978	1990	2002	2014
Sheep	1943	1955	1967	1979	1991	2003	2015
Monkey	1944	1956	1968	1980	1992	2004	2016
Cock	1945	1957	1969	1981	1993	2005	2017
Dog	1946	1958	1970	1982	1994	2006	2018
Pig	1947	1959	1971	1983	1995	2007	2019

According to junishi-do-jutsu, each yearly animal totem has a strongest and a weakest time of the day, corresponding to a period of two Western hours. For example, for a person born under the sign of the Cock the strongest period of the day is from 5 p.m. to 7 p.m. Moving toward this period, in ascendancy, the Cock steadily gains in strength. Moving away from this prime time, toward its 11 a.m. to 1 p.m. latency period, the Cock becomes weaker and more vulnerable to both physical and mental assault.

Mind-slayers employing junishi-do-jutsu also take into consideration the foe's weakest time of day in order to determine when the target will be most susceptible to the power of suggestion.

Another factor is whether or not the foe is surrounded by conflicting (toxic) birth beasts that draw off his energy, rather than complimenting birth beasts that strengthen him. A Cock, for example, will have trouble working with or marrying someone born under a Horse sign.

When infiltrating a kuniochi agent into an enemy court, ninja strategists were careful to pick a female agent whose birth beast made her compatible with, and hence more attractive to, the targeted foe.

The Weaknesses of the Beasts

Medieval ninja diligently catalogued the inherent weaknesses associated with each birth-totem of Chinese astrology.

The Cock

The Cock, for example, has a strong point when it comes to being punctual. However, that same punctuality—or predictability—can make a Cock more vulnerable to a wily ninja assassin. (Musashi warns against being predictable, even to the point of never having a favorite weapon or even footwork one favors.)

Combative, eccentric, and often selfish, Cocks like the public eye. Still, they can be secretly insecure and in need of constant bolstering—opening the door for the insincere praise of a "sympathetic" mind-slayer.

The Cock is a perfectionist who can't admit to being wrong and is thus easily trapped by the mind-slayer who first makes the Cock appear wrong and then provides him a way out of being wrong. This two-pronged ploy follows classic Chinese strategy. Says Tu Mu:

> "Trap an already trapped foe twice by offering him a clear road to safety, creating the possibility for life where before there was only the determination of death. Having done so, strike!"

The Dog

The Dog is loyal to a fault, that fault being that, at the extreme, Dog-dominated people are born followers, and easily led astray by others. Dogs are also generous, making them prime targets for donation scams, especially from religious hucksters who use "plain talk."

The Pig

The Pig lives for today and has a dangerous "fatalistic" streak. The Pig is home-loving (which can lead to laziness) and is also family-oriented. Thus, Pigs marry early and, as a result, are prone to marital strife. Mind-slayers get to the Pig through his/her spouse.

The Rat

The Rat is ambitious and a hard worker who refuses to ask for help or take charity. Thus pride cometh before his fall. The Rat seldom makes lasting friendships. Thus the mind-slayer undermines the Rat by targeting his small circle of friends.

The Ox

The Ox is a complainer. Feigning sympathy for his bitching gets you close to him. The Ox tries to live up to the expectations of others. Show him a way to do this, or make him doubt that he is accomplishing this, and you will have the Ox's undivided attention.

The Tiger

The Tiger is candid to the point of rudeness. Restless, rebellious, and suspicious, the Tiger keeps his promises and becomes angry with those who do not. Feeling betrayed, he may react violently. We can imagine the title character in *Othello* being a Tiger.

The Rabbit

The Rabbit is kind and sensitive, making him the perfect patsy for sympathy ploys. The Rabbit becomes frustrated and doesn't think straight when inconvenienced. He hates to fight, and thus is prone to compromise. For the most part, Rabbits are shy, yet are good in business and handle money well. A business venture that "needs" his expertise will get the Rabbit to open his door every time. For all their business savvy, Rabbits believe in luck.

Thus, the mind-slayer arranges for a windfall that becomes the Rabbit's downfall.

The Dragon

The Dragon thinks he's above the law. Eccentric like the Cock, Dragon expects admiration. Dragon has an explosive temper, and is passionate about nature and his health.

The Dragon is so energetic that, like a fire which is continuously fanned higher and higher, Dragons often burn out early in life and are consumed on a pyre of their own energies.

Martial arts great Bruce Lee was born in 1940, year of the Dragon at the hour of the Dragon, making him a "Double Dragon," a very powerful celestial sign in the East. A restless, noisy, and temperamental child, the

Bruce Lee the world came to admire was in every way a Dragon personality: passionate about health, somewhat eccentric, and in many ways feeling himself above the law in the way he readily revealed many Eastern martial arts secrets to the West.

The Snake

The Snake is attracted by physical beauty and thus is susceptible to the finer things in life. Vain and high-tempered, a Snake-dominated personality is ripe for lust-seduction ploys.

For example, a male Snake will become putty in the hands of a kuniochi, while a vain female-Snake can be trapped with promises of the fountain of youth.

Do not underestimate the Snake, however. Snakes can be calculating and ruthless. Snakes are also poor gamblers and superstitious. The Snake's biggest failing is that he can't let an opportunity pass. Thus, he has no way of knowing when those two raps on his door will be from Death disguised as opportunity!

The Horse

The Horse likes to be the center of attention and needs people (thus, approach the Horse in the guise of an adoring fan). Ostentatious and impatient, Horse often suffers from restlessness and insomnia.

The Sheep

The Sheep is timid and prefers anonymity, but is quick to defend the underdog, making him susceptible to sympathy ploys.

The Sheep has trouble handling personal criticism. As a result, Sheep lets pressure build up. When Sheep finally does explode, it is with inappropriate anger. (It is not a good idea for a Sheep-dominated person to get a job as a postal worker!)

Rather than arranging major trauma stressors in a Sheep's life, the mind-slayer attacks the Sheep in small increments, increasing the pressure little-by-little until the Sheep explodes.

The Monkey

The Monkey is always full of plans, and always looking for someone (like an attentive mind-slayer) to tell those plans to.

Innovators and inventors, the Monkeys are nonetheless easily discouraged and confused, and thus open to anyone (such as a mind-slayer) who acts like he knows the answer.[2]

Conclusion

Your order of birth and your birth beast can have positive and negative influences on your life. These two factors are predispositions, not predestination, and point only to innate tendencies that once aware of, we are free to embrace or reject.

The more we study The Five Weaknesses, the Eight Relationships, the Nine Roles, and the 12 Beasts that mind-slayers use to manipulate and master others, the better our skill at avoiding being mastered ourselves!

The master and those mastered . . . the former depends on prior study, the latter, on lack of prior study.

ENDNOTES

1. Lung, Haha. *Assassin! Secrets of the Cult of Assassins*. Boulder, Colorado: Paladin Press, 1997.
2. For more on junishi-do-jutsu, see: Lung, Haha. *The Ninja Craft*. Boulder, Colorado: Paladin Press, 1997.

CHAPTER 4

SECRETS OF THE SENNIN

"Use your imagination before
you are forced to use your desperation!"
—Ralf Dean Omar,
*Death on Your Doorstep:
101 Weapons in the Home*

Down through the ages, countless schools of thought—both mystical and secular—have sought explanations for how the mind functions and what motivates human beings.

From shamans to Buddha, from ancient soothsayers to modern psychiatrists, many have tried to take apart the human mind with methods ranging from reading animal entrails and tea leaves to modern electronic devices. Many undertake this search in order to better understand themselves and benefit others. Others—mind-slayers—use the insights of the ancients and the inventions of modern researchers to control—and kill—others.

Modern psychology only confirms what the ancients deduced intuitively: that human beings can have either a positive or a negative outlook on life, that humans have different motivations for their actions, and that we all function at different levels of awareness and understanding.

Yet mind-slayers are quick to realize the most important thing about human beings: For all our uniqueness, for all our seeming differences, we are all strikingly similar. Thus, things like how we think, our body language, even our patterns of speech, all make us susceptible to The Black Science of mind-slayers who are masters at manipulating those fears and dark secrets we all hold close to our chests. Close enough that a dagger of the mind piercing them may well plunge all the way to our hearts!

Before they could successfully overshadow—influence and control a foe—ninja sennin had to determine how that foe viewed the world.

59

How we perceive the world greatly influences our self-concept. In turn, our self-concept determines how we deal with the world.

HALF-EMPTY OR HALF-FULL

Determining a person's overall outlook on life, whether he is optimistic or pessimistic, whether he maintains a positive or negative outlook, is vital in determining a mind-slayer's approach to that individual.

- Does he see life as basically good or bad, the glass half full or half empty?
- Is he internally motivated or externally oriented?
- Does he have true self-worth stemming from genuine personal, social, and educational accomplishments, or does he instead define himself by externals such as racial identity, cult affiliation, or gang membership. All these are superficial factors easily manipulated by unscrupulous mind-slayers.
- Does he feel himself in control of his destiny or does he see himself as a victim molded, traumatized, and at the mercy of his environment?
- Is he a slave to what he's been taught, chained by positions and prejudices inherited from intolerant racial and religious ancestors?
- What myths, excuses, and defense mechanisms does he cling to as part of his identity?
- Does he believe that gods or leaders will shepherd him to salvation and success (tariki), or that only through his own self-effort (jiriki) will his safety be guaranteed?

In order to understand the innate motivations nature blesses (or burdens) an individual with, medieval ninja used observation and studied such disciplines as Chinese astrology and the I Ching. They also observed the role nurture plays in the development and motivations of individuals by studying family and social interactions through such sciences as pakua.

UNDERMINING SELF-CONCEPT AND IDENTITY

Someone once said there are three ways we are seen: how we see ourselves, how others see us, and how we really are!

Self-Concept

Our self-concept is a mirror reflecting the beliefs we hold about ourselves. Some are true, many are fantasies or wishful thinking. This includes the likes and dislikes that make us similar to, or different from, others.

Self-concept keeps track of how we see ourselves and where we see ourselves in the great scheme of things. Our self-concept also includes the amount of confidence we have in our ability to face challenges.

For mind-slayers, undermining a foe's positive self-image and confidence is job one. Once his confidence is undermined, the walls of that foe's mind castle come crashing down!

Much of our identity grows from our interaction with others. This is why cults and dictatorships limit access to outside sources of information and restrict interaction with anyone other than approved cult sources. To say "I don't care what others think!" is as naive as it is dangerous.

Ninja warriors knew the importance of at least appearing invincible in order to discourage attack on both self and clan. Thus the ancient adage that "Reputation spills less blood."

The Quest for Identity

Some us identify with positive family role models such as honored parents or respected relatives. Others model themselves after teachers or religious leaders. Further afield, some imitate the dress and deportment of cultural heroes and celebrities. Still others embrace "anti-identities" by emulating criminals and by joining pariah cults.

Cults and gangs are notorious for giving recruits new identities: new names, a new language (cult speak and gang codes), and a distinctive and often disruptive manner of dress designed to further isolate the recruit from non-cult members. Such ready-made identities are seductive, especially for the young and the gullible who lack a clearly defined genuine identity of their own.

Our present reactions to people and situations are to a great extent merely a repeat of our past reactions. Repeating these same reactions over and over becomes our identity. The first time we encounter a sensation our brain records its initial reaction to that sensation and files that reaction away for future reference. In subsequent encounters with similar sensations, we recall these past sensation-reactions in order to determine our present reaction. Here then is the root of all prejudice and phobia.

Our identity is thus a record of our reactions to past sensations, and our identification with—and attachment to—those past reactions.

Knowing that past reactions make up the bulk of a victim's identity, mind-slayers try to learn all they can about a targeted victim's past behavior (reactions). This makes it all the easier for the mind-slayer to anticipate and manipulate that victim's future behavior. Thus, a mind-slayer reminding us of a past failure can make us hesitate in the present.

Let's say a person is planning to do business with a competitor of yours and you know the person has a phobia of rats. Prior to the person meeting your competitor the first time, you have a conversation with the person where you subtly (but repeatedly) mention the fact that your competitor's toupee looks "small and furry." If your competitor lacks a toupee, mention how he has "ferret-like eyes," and use other rat-like adjectives to describe your competitor.

Mind-slayers attack identity (self-worth, etc.) looking for chinks in their victim's mental armor. The more vulnerable points the mind-slayer spots in a foe's defenses, all the easier to ply The Black Science on them.

THE 10 MINDS (JUJUSHIN)

According to Japanese Buddhist Master Kukai (774-835 CE), there are 10 basic levels of understanding and awareness at which all humans function. Buddhists use each of the "10 Minds" (*jujushin*) as stepping stones to enlightenment. For ninja mind-slayers, on the other hand, the jujushin is just another stumbling block to place in the path of a foe.

These 10 Minds are: Goat's Mind, Fool's Mind, Child's Mind, Dead Man's Mind, No-Karma Mind, Compassionate Mind, Unborn Mind; Single-Truth Mind, No-Self Mind, and Secret Mind. Each of the 10 Minds contains the seed of the others.

Although we may normally function at one of the higher levels, it is always possible at any given moment to slip (or be pushed) back "down" to a lower, more primal, level of thinking.

Mind-slayers, of course, purposely try to force their victims to function at the lowest, hence simplest and most easily manipulated, level possible. The ability to recognize which of the 10 Minds a foe is operating at helps mind-slayers devise strategies individually tailored to that foe.

JUJUSHIN: THE 10 MINDS

Level	His outlook	His weakness/your approach
Goat's Mind	Has potential for growth. Literal thinker.	Lusts for food and sex. Has no understanding of cause and effect. Feed his appetites till he chokes.
Fool's Mind	Strives to be moral. Fears punishment from man and God. Believes in ritual.	Socially influenced, motivated by fear. Has some understanding of cause and effect. Show him how to clear his conscience.
Child's Mind	Religious. Literal-minded.	Seeks approval outside self (gangs, religion, etc.). Give him a uniform and he'll follow you anywhere.
Dead Man's Mind	Worries about dying. Worries about the future.	Builds "immortality projects"— businesses and broods that will live on beyond him. Show him how to "live forever."
No-Karma Mind	Understands cause and effect, lawful	Justice obsessed. Follows the letter of the law and believes in an eye for an eye. Help him indict himself.
Compassion Mind	Feels mercy and compassion for others.	Easily trapped with sympathy ploys.
Unborn Mind	Believes in fate, God, and luck.	Can be fatalistic. Often not in touch with the real world. Feed his fantasies. Let him win the first few hands.
Single-Truth Mind	Cerebral.	Can be amoral and believes the end justifies the means. Has feelings of false clarity. Praise his insight.
No-Self Mind	Sees beyond self, thinks of others first.	Trap him with a "good cause" and with sympathy ploys.
Secret Mind	Non-attached. Self-sufficient	Do not approach directly. Use a cutting-at-the-edges ploy.

SHADOW LANGUAGE

"For by his face straight shall you know his heart."
—Shakespeare, *King Richard III*

It has been estimated that as much as 70 percent of all communication between people is carried on without the use of words, through our body language (posture, gestures, movement, etc.). Even when we do use words to communicate, a large percentage of our communication is not through the actual words spoken, but rather our tone, patterns of speech, and the types of words we favor to convey our meaning.

Mind-slayers call this our "shadow language" and study its subtlety in order to, first, guard themselves against detection, and second, to better manipulate others.

Betrayed by the Body

"There's no art to find the mind's construction in the face."
—Shakespeare, *Macbeth*

The mind-slayer's Black Science is as much muscle-reading as it is mind-reading.

Medieval ninja relied on being able to read the body language of others in order to spot approaching danger. In addition, as part of their sixth training hall (art of disguise), ninja mastered nuances of posture, walk, and gesture in order to disguise their own body language.

One of the skills taught in the ninth hall of ninjutsu (art of mysticism) was how to disguise your *wa* (spirit, presence, intention) when approaching a foe. Musashi also lectured at length on the importance of studying "attitude," i.e. the body language that betrays one's intent.

Modern self-defense experts also know the importance of both reading the body language of others as well as learning to project their own body language into an "attitude" of confidence intended to dissuade attack.[1]

Reading the Body-Book

The "body-type determines behavior" theory was first put forth by the Greek Hippocrates (circa 460-370 BCE). Down through the ages various half-baked theories about physiognomy—the art of determining personality through observing physical appearance—have been proposed.

At different times various physiognomy-based prejudices and stereotypes have been believed. For example, it was once believed criminals could be identified by their beady little eyes, sloping foreheads, and their lack of earlobes. In the 1940s and '50s, psychology researchers claimed they could determine a person's overall personality by classifying them into one of three somatotypes:

Ectomorphs are tall, thin, and poorly muscled. They tend to be brainy—your basic nerd stereotype. Mesomorphs are short and stocky and have a lot of muscle. They tend to be more physical-minded. Endomorphs are round-faced and fat. Big surprise, these people were thought to be more sedentary and lazy.

We still maintain many of these stereotypes/prejudices:

- Fat people are jolly;
- People with high foreheads are deep thinkers;
- Blondes are dumb; and
- The size of a man's nose is directly proportionate to his . . . you get the idea.

Yet even without formal training, it is simple for most of us to determine when someone is happy or depressed, excited or bored, simply by looking at his or her body language:

Walking: Is his step light (carefree) or shuffling (weary, concerned)?

Posture: Is his spine straight (confident, alert, determined) or slouching (tired, defeated)?

Head angle: Is his chin up (determined, defiant) or downcast (passive, guilty)?

> "Your face, my thane, is as a book where men
> May read strange matters."
> —Shakespeare, *Macbeth*

The Face: The Kama Sutra advises that among the arts to be studied if you really want to be good at manipulating others is "the art of knowing the character of a man from his features."

All of us can easily spot the 10 basic emotions on another's face: joy, anger, interest/excitement, disgust, surprise, contempt, sadness, fear, shame, and guilt. We can also tell much from the movement of hands: Are his knuckles clenched white in stress or anger? Are his fingers drumming in nervousness or impatience? Wringing in worry? All of these non-verbal indicators are "tells," or unconscious body language signals we all give off.

"Tells" include such easy-to-spot clues as blushing (from guilt or embarrassment), indications of lying (fidgeting, sweaty palms), and signs of fear (pale face, trembling). Other body "tells" include changes in breathing, direct eye contact (or lack of), and physical tension (muscle tics, fingering objects, etc.). Speech "tells" include stuttering, hesitations, and Freudian slips of the tongue.

Personal distance: Another simple body language tell is distancing, which refers to how close individuals stand to one another. Casual conversation takes place with individuals standing three to five feet from one another. Closer than this is known as intimate distance and indicates either confiding or conspiracy conversation.

The distance between people can even help us pin down a person's culture of origin. Anglo-Americans are generally more space- and distance-defensive and less touch-oriented than many cultures. Middle Easterners, for example, stand closer than Americans when talking—close enough to feel one another's breath (and to note one another's breathing patterns) and read one another's eyes. Men in other cultures embrace and kiss upon meeting, something pretty much taboo in North America.

Gestures: Gesture "tells" include rubbing the body and smoothing out wrinkles in clothing (and in the lies they are telling). The unconscious tapping together of a person's thumb and index finger (making the "OK" sign) can be a tell that person secretly wants to agree with you, if only to avoid an argument. Palms unconsciously flapping out from the body can indicate "I don't know." That almost imperceptible shrug the person is unaware he is doing may be an indication he is unsure about what he is talking about and/or has subconscious doubts.

If you doubt the power of simple gestures, watch how "flipping the bird" can change the mood of a whole room full of people!

Gestures also vary in meaning from place to place.

The American two-finger "V for victory" (palm outward) gesture, when turned with palm inward, means "screw you!" in some countries, including Australia. (You may recall the uproar a visiting President George Bush caused when he flashed a cheering Aussie crowd what he thought was the "V for victory" sign—palm inward!)

Watchers, Listeners, and Touchers

Mind-slayers classify people into three types, depending on their primary mode of gathering information:

- Watchers are dominated by what they see;
- Listeners are ruled by what they hear; and
- Touchers process information primarily through their senses of touch and taste.

We all use these three, but each of us tend to favor one style of information-gathering more and this becomes a vital component to our personality.

Don't worry, you won't have to guess whether people are watchers, listeners, or touchers. They will tell you in a half dozen ways:

Watch What They Do

Watchers' minds tend to wander when listening to others talk. They like to read. They have good handwriting, doodle while thinking, and are good spellers (although they often need to actually write the word out or close their eyes to recall what words look like).

Watchers are good at remembering faces (but not names). They notice details (like your lodge pin and college ring). Watchers collect paintings, baseball cards, and comic books.

When rewarding a watcher, give him a plaque or a degree he can hang across from his desk and look at every day.

Listeners enjoy talking. Sometimes they talk, sing, or hum to themselves. They like music and often collect records. Like watchers, listeners remember faces well. Listeners enjoy listening activities, from music to poetry read aloud.

Listeners enjoy wordplay and verbal riddles. They are easily captivated by a good talker. Reward a listener with concert tickets or a new CD.

Touchers like rewards they can touch (trophies, for example). As the name implies, touchers like to touch others when talking and physically handle objects when working.

Touchers use their hands when talking and tend to tap their pencils and bounce their feet while studying. They are poor spellers. They enjoy physically challenging work. They like taking engines apart and putting puzzles together.

Observe Their Breathing

Watchers breathe high in the chest. Listeners breathe evenly from mid-chest. Touchers breathe from their bellies.

Watch Their Heads

Watchers keep their chins up, trying to see as much as possible. Listeners keep their heads balanced or cocked to one ear or the other. Head down with neck muscles relaxed usually indicates a toucher.

Listen to the Words They Choose

The verbal imagery we employ betrays us as watchers, listeners, or touchers.

VERBAL IMAGERY THAT BETRAYS US

Watchers	Listeners	Touchers
See	Hear	Touch (base)
Look	Listen	Grasp (concept or meaning)
View	Sound	Concrete
Appear	Harmonize	Heavy
Show	Tune in/out	Intense
Mind's eye	Soft-spoken	Tap into
Crystal clear	Loud and clear	Vibes
Short-sighted	Tongue-tied	Hands down
"I see your point"	"I'm all ears"	"I'm not following you."

Where a toucher will say, "Someone must be talking about me; my ears are burning," a listener says "My ears are ringing." The same newspaper headlines that "scream" for listeners "jump out" at touchers.

Rather than making a decision based on only one or two descriptive words used by a person, mind-slayers look for patterns of speech that reveal a person favoring one form of verbal imagery over the others.

Watchers process the world through their eyes: "He was short with me," "That's certainly a tall order." For watchers, a person is "positively glowing," "radiant," or a "shining" example to others. Words are "beautiful," the boss in an "ugly" mood.

Listeners hear an office "buzzing" with gossip, a room "humming" with excitement. A name often "rings" a bell.

Touchers use direction (describing their mood as "up," "down," or "low") and temperature (describing people as "cold," receptions "chilly," and lovers "hot"). Touchers use tactile-oriented words describing others as "a hard nut to crack" or "a smooth operator." In dealing with others, touchers chide themselves for being too "soft," other times too "rough."

Using movement imagery, touchers describe attitudes ("keeping one's head above water"), intent ("trying to sway the jury," "waiting for the other shoe to drop"), and actions ("give him the brush-off").

A dead giveaway is when touchers get "vibes" and actually interject the word "feel" into their speech: "It just feels wrong to me," "We don't feel as close as we used to," "I have a feel for business," and "a feel for the game."

The Eyes Have It

Someone once said the eyes are the windows of the soul. Hyperbole perhaps, but it is true that a person's eyes can give an alert mind-slayer all the information needed to manipulate that person.

Beyond our control, our eyes widen in surprise, narrow in suspicion. Arab businessmen wear sunglasses when negotiating so as not to tip their hands by displaying interest when their pupils dilate.

Mind-slayers know that 90 percent of people look up and to the left when remembering, up and right when creating images in their minds. In simplest terms: Left = memory, Right = imagining and creating. By watching where a person's eyes go when asked a question, we can discern whether he is being truthful or lying.

For example, we look up and to the left when remembering something we saw, such as a picture. Conversely, we look up and to the right when daydreaming or creating a picture—or creating a lie.

We look to the side for sounds—to the left to recall a tune and to the right when trying to imagine what something might sound like.

We look down when recalling things we touched, tasted, or smelled, and sometimes when recalling emotional hurt. Thus we look left and down to recall the feel or smell of leather, down and right to imagine what something might feel, smell, or taste like. (Here's a mnemonic aid: We hang pictures up on a wall; our ears are to the sides; and when depressed, we feel down.)

For another way to figure out if a person is a watcher, a listener, or a toucher, try a variation of the following exercise. Ask the person questions you know he knows the answers to, then note where his eyes go looking for the answer.

Question: "What model was the first car you owned?" Responding, he looks up and to the left, recalling the picture of the car in his mind.
Question: "Do you remember what the radio sounded like?" Responding, he looks left and to the side, searching for a remembered sound.
Question: "What kind of seats did it have, leather or fabric?" Responding, he looks left and down, remembering the feel of the seat.

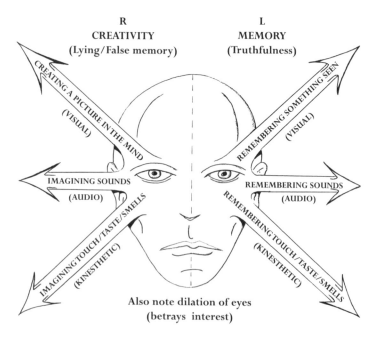

70

Question: "Can you imagine what a car would be like if it didn't have wheels and instead flew?" Responding, he looks up and to the right, creating a picture in his mind.

Question: "What would a flying car's engine sound like?" Responding, he looks to right side, trying to imagine the sound.

Question: "Do you think a ride in such a car would be bumpy or smooth?" He looks right and down, trying to imagine what it would feel like.

Note: These directions are reversed for about 10 percent of people, most often lefties. When encountering such a person, use the same strategy, simply reversing directions.

Mind-slayers can quickly test whether a potential victim is a watcher, listener, or a toucher in order to tailor their approach to that victim.

For example, when dealing with a toucher, don't talk a mile a minute and don't waste your time describing how something looks to him. Instead, let the toucher feel, smell, or taste the product. Even if you're trying to sell him a piece of land three states away, bring him a sample of the soil or a pinecone from the site to touch and smell.

When debating, in order to frustrate your opponent, deliberately switch styles on him. If he is a toucher, confuse him with vivid visual descriptions, wall charts, and descriptive metaphors.

When confronted by two individuals with differing information gathering styles, you can drive a wedge between them by choosing a style favored by one but not the other. Thus you kill two birds with one stone, freezing one of them out of the conversation, while praising the other for being smart enough to understand what you are saying.

Betrayed by a Whisper

Words are power. Every day people live and die by single words spoken. It is said a man begins by telling you what he knows and if you let him talk long enough, he'll start telling you what he doesn't know!

Mind-slayers study both the speech styles and patterns of speech of potential victims in order to better mimic those styles and patterns. Other times, mind-slayers purposely choose contra-styles and patterns of speaking they know will confuse their victim.

The Three Types of "Shit"

According to Fritz Perls (1893-1970), founder of the Gestalt school of psychology, there are three kinds of shit you are likely to run into while talking with people:

- Chicken-shit is clichéd small talk, devoid of actual information content, small talk that avoids emotional contact.
- Bull-shit refers to out-and-out lies. All lies are told for one of three reasons: to conceal the truth and cover wrong-doing, to protect someone, and/or in order to gain (money, prestige, sex, etc.).
- Elephant-shit refers to grandiose plans that avoid confronting reality and responsibility. For example, telling people what you'll do when you win the lottery.

Mind-slayers become adept at using all three of these types of "verbal shit" in order to woo their audience. They also learn to spot what kind of verbal shit a potential victim favors, since this tells the mind-slayer a lot about the victim's personality:

Chicken-shitters are fearful of human contact, and often harbor secrets by which they can be extorted. Bull-shitters are opportunists. They will lie to promote themselves and their agenda. Elephant-shitters are full of plans that have no hope of ever coming true. These types can be approached with the promise to help make those dreams come true. Other Elephant-shitters are approached by reinforcing their victim identity, telling them something like, "You could have done better if so many people hadn't been against you."

Matching Speech Patterns

In order to get closer to a victim, mind-slayers first discover and then imitate the speech patterns of their targeted victims.

Watchers tend to speak quickly (trying to describe the images they see in their mind's eye). Their minds stray during long lectures. When trying to win them over, be short and to the point.

Listeners are more selective about the words they use and tend to have more tone-rich voices. Their speech is slower, more rhythmic and measured. Since words mean a lot to them, they are careful what they say. Listeners are quick to pick up on that intentional "slip of the tongue" and that influential name you intentionally drop.

Touchers are even slower in speech than watchers and listeners. They tend to have deeper voices and to speak smoothly.

Tone. The tone of speech a person uses, as well as the type of words he employs, says more than the actual words spoken. Nearly 40 percent of our communication comes not from the words we speak but from the tone of speech used.

For example, quiet tones can indicate fear, conspiracy, or intimacy. Loud, forceful tones can indicate confidence, or false bravado. Terse speech is used for scolding others and indicates impatience. Soothing tones calm and heal.

Speech Content. In addition to listening to how people talk, it is important to listen to what people talk about.

Women tend to talk more about close things: family, health, sex, weight, food, and clothing. Men on the other hand are more comfortable talking about at-a-safer-distance things—neutral topics such as sports, news, and politics.

When attempting to establish rapport with another person, for example when inducing a hypnotic state, mind-slayers first identify the person's dominant speech patterns—tone and type. Then they tailor their own speech accordingly with words and phrases of similar tone and type designed to make the targeted person feel at ease.

Mirroring
"Many things can be passed on. Both sleepiness and yawning can
be passed on. Time can also be passed on."
—Miyamoto Musashi

When you generate familiarity, trust, and comfort in others, they become more receptive to your ideas and are more willing to help you accomplish your goals.

Doctors call establishing this kind of initial rapport their "bedside manner." Salesmen and Jehovah's Witnesses call it "getting a foot in the door." Mind-slayers call it mirroring, or "the beginning of the end."

To establish rapport with another person, whether he is a potential customer or an enemy you are trying to "rock to sleep," pay close attention to him.

Listen to what he says, but also to how he says it.

Watch how he moves, his body language, and how he sits.

When sitting with him, adopt an open posture with your elbows away from your body with your legs stretched out, rather than a closed position where your elbows are close to your body and your knees together.

Smile as much as possible. (Note: You can spot a fake smile because it is switched on more abruptly than a genuine smile and is generally held longer, about four to five seconds.)

Make direct eye contact and begin mirroring the person you are trying to persuade. Adjust your gestures, tempo and tone of your voice, and body positioning to mirror his. Imitate his distinctive movements and body positioning (sitting upright versus lounging relaxed).

Be careful not to appear mocking.

Once you determine whether the person is a watcher, listener, or a toucher, pepper your speech with his favored phrases ("I see . . .", "I hear . . .", I feel . . ."), purposely tailoring your speech to excite him.

The purpose of mirroring (sometimes called matching) is to convince another person you are just like him. Once you have convinced him of this, once in synch with the other person, you can then begin manipulating the pace, tone, and direction of your communication, gently leading the conversation where you want it to go.

The more attention we pay to the whispers of our enemy's shadow language today, the better our chances to avoid hearing our own screams tomorrow!

ENDNOTE

1. Skinner, Dirk. *Street Ninja: Ancient Secrets for Surviving Today's Mean Streets*. New York: Barricade Books, 1995.

CHAPTER 5

THE BLACK SCIENCE

"In the course of history, human beings
have evolved a truly amazing number of
ways to manipulate one another."
—Gerald W. Piaget, Ph.D.,
*Control Freaks: Who They Are and How
to Stop Them from Running Your Life*

Responsible for guarding the collective mind castle of their clan, ninja sennin crafted a virtual science of psychological insights and techniques, all designed to benefit their clan.

Of course, in the shadow realm of the shinobi, a good blade cuts both ways.

Not surprising then that this same benign collection of helpful psychological insights should be added to the Black Science of the mind-slayer!

The catalogue of this Black Science consists of defensive and offensive psychological warfare ploys that allow mind-slayers to first penetrate into a foe's mind and, once there, do as much damage as possible!

USES OF SUPERSTITION

"Often the best cloak in which to wrap yourself
is your enemy's superstition,
the best of masks to hide behind, your enemy's fear."
—Dr. Haha Lung, *The Ninja Craft*

The more unstable the times, the more precarious a people's existence, the more they cling to superstitions. While most superstitions are harmless, some superstitions open us to physical danger and mental manipulation.

A superstition should not be confused with spiritual beliefs and practices. Spiritual practice has—or should have—a basis somewhere in fact. Superstitions, on the other hand, are unfounded personal or cultural-religious beliefs that spring from either the misinterpretation of an actual occurrence or simply from wishful thinking. A simpler definition is that "superstition" is what we call the other guy's religion. (Our religion is, of course, The Truth!)

Superstitions abound worldwide and vary from culture to culture.

In the West, number "13" is unlucky, while in the East, it is the number "four," because the word for "four," "shi," is a homonym of the word for "death" in both Chinese and Japanese. In the West, breaking a mirror is seven years bad luck. In Russia it is bad luck to give a mirror as a gift, but in Japan a mirror is an honored gift, one of the three sacred Imperial objects.

Kyonin-No-Jutsu
"Let pale-faced fear keep with the mean-born man,
And find no harbor in a royal heart."
—Shakespeare, *2 King Henry VI*

The deadly and arbitrary nature of medieval Japanese warfare ensured that the majority of samurai clung stubbornly to traditional beliefs in ancient shamanism, Shinto mythology, and the power of esoteric chants and spells (jomon) designed to protect them from sickness and death.

Many 12th century samurai worshipped the warrior-demon Fudo. And even though most of the samurai and even the emperors of the time practiced Buddhist meditation, they often did so only as a superstitious means of exorcising evil spirits (*kami*), rather than as a tool for enlightenment. This samurai "superstitious streak" was not lost on their enemies, the ninja.

Ninja sennin understood that knowing what superstitions a foe invests in provides invaluable insight into that foe's behavior. Thus ninja sennin developed kyonin-no-jutsu, the art of using one's beliefs and superstition against him.

Ninja Use of Superstition
The most important of kyonin-no-jutsu ploys used by the shinobi was their encouragement of the belief that their clans had descended from the

storm-god Susano via mysterious *tengu* demons, thus superstitiously linking the shinobi with the darker side of divinity. Also known as *kinjin* (goblins), tengu lived in clans, each clan ruled by a *jonin* chieftain. When they allowed themselves to be seen, tengu appeared as part-man, part-bird, long-beaked, and winged.

Tengu are either black or red in color and are master shape-shifters. When appearing in human form, they appear as little men wearing short cloaks (made of feathers, leaves, or straw) and wearing large black hats. Tengu were great swordsmen and possessed powers of magic and invisibility.

Whether medieval ninja actually believed themselves to be descended from tengu, or whether they simply encouraged the myth in order to further instill fear in their foes, is a moot point. What matters is the strategy worked and medieval ninja were neither the first nor the last secretive group to use the ploy. Throughout history, secretive societies have purposely woven tales about their being descended from demons or fierce animal spirits in order to feed the fears and superstitions of the foes:

- Chinese Kung-fu martial artists claim their "unbeatable" fighting styles derived from animals;
- The Leopard Cult, terrorizing West Africa up into the 20th century, encouraged the belief they were the spawn of vengeful leopard spirits sent to cleanse the land of Europeans. To perpetuate this myth, they outfitted themselves with leopard skins and wielded claw-like weapons;
- Viking Berserkers and Wolfshirts wore the skins of their respective animal totems and imitated those beasts' styles of fighting; the Berserks ("Bear-shirts") whipping themselves into a ferocious battle frenzy, and Wolfshirts adopting the wily ninja-like ways of the wolf-spirit;
- Native American warrior lodges also linked themselves spiritually (and superstitiously, in the minds of their foes) with various animal totems (eagle, bear, snake, etc.);
- Hashishin (assassins) of the Middle East encouraged the belief they were descended from demon jinn "genie"[1] and
- The Thuggee Stranglers of India encouraged both enemy and initiate to believe they were actual "Faithful Tigers" who had been given human form by the dark Goddess Kali:

> "Walking around the circle of tigers counterclock-
> wise, one by one, Kali-ma raised the nine fierce tigers
> up as men. . . . When she finished walking completely
> around the circle, where once had stood nine fierce
> tigers, now stood the first nine Thugs!"[2]

One ninja-trained warrior who wielded superstition like a fine sword was 12th century samurai hero Yoshitsune, who did nothing to stop the spread of stories that he'd been schooled by tengu demons.

Yoshitsune founded the karuma-hachi school of martial arts responsible for teaching the guerilla (i.e. ninjutsu) tactics that helped his Minimoto clan defeat their enemies. Through Yoshitsune's efforts, his brother Yoritomo became Japan's first shogun in 1192.

No sooner had Yoritomo ascended to power than he began killing anyone he imagined posed a threat to his absolute rule. A superstitious paranoid, Yoritomo performed daily cleansing rituals designed to prevent the angry ghosts of those he'd killed from returning to haunt him. Eventually Yoritomo turned to killing even those loyal to him, and Yoshitsune was forced to flee.

Some say Yoshitsune was eventually murdered by Yoritomo's agents, others that Yoshitsune committed hari-kiri rather than be taken captive. According to shinobi lore however, Yoshitsune used his ninja skills to escape to China, but not before getting revenge against his evil brother.

Shortly after Yoshitsune's reported death, small, inexplicable incidents began happening to Yoritomo.

Objects belonging to his dead brother began appearing and often Yoritomo would hear Yoshitsune's voice from behind a screen, yet when the screen was jerked aside no one was there!

Yoritomo, an accomplished rider, died in 1198 after a fall from his horse. Critically injured, the shogun lingered in agony for days and died screaming to his last breath that he had been attacked by the ghost of his dead brother!

Shinobi lore tells it this way: Yoshitsune first faked his death and then began harassing his brother by making Yoritomo believe he was being haunted by the restless ghost of the brother he had unjustly killed. This kyonin-no-jutsu campaign culminated in the "ghost" of Yoshitsune (Yoshitsune himself or a confederate) suddenly "materializing" before his already frazzled brother during Yoritomo's evening ride.

Of course, ninja are not the only ones to use superstition as a weapon.

Voodoo and Bone-Pointing
"Although methods differ, the magic works
when there is sufficient belief in its power."
—*Mysteries of the Unexplained*

Many primitive peoples believe that through spells, rituals, hexes, and curses a person can wound or even kill another. (While this might seem like mindless superstition to our more "advanced" sensibilities, stop and think for a moment how many of us regularly pray for health, healing, and tomorrow's lottery numbers.)

Australian Aborigines use "bone-pointing" to strike down foes from a distance. Basically, a curse is placed on a symbolic weapon made of bone, wood, or stone and when this weapon is pointed at the victim or touches the victim, illness and death occur in a short time unless a counterspell is administered by the *nangarri* (medicine man).

Most in the West are familiar with Caribbean voodoo. The popular idea of a voodoo priest sticking pins in a doll in order to cause the illness or death of an enemy may seem farfetched to non-believers, but is taken quite seriously amongst voodoo believers. Therein lies its power.

While the bulk of voodoo practice is aimed at healing, as in all religions there are always those few mind-slayers who use the faithfuls' beliefs against them. This is known in voodoo as the "Work of the Left Hand" and includes death spells and the creation of zombies, both often accomplished through the use of poisons.[3]

Each voodoo priest or priestess is also a *dokte fey* (master herbalist). Thus voodoo priests are adept at using drugs in addition to sleight-of-hand and symbolism to mimic true magical powers. When the faithful are convinced a voodoo priest possesses great power (*mojo*) and/or is favored by the spirits, that voodoo priest (i.e. mind-slayer) is much feared.

(Note: In Louisiana, in the 1980s, a man got life in prison for contracting a voodoo priest to put a death spell on his enemy. The judge instructed the jury that it didn't matter if *they* (the jury) didn't believe in the power of voodoo to kill from a distance, because the *defendant* believed he was hiring a magical hitman!)

How Fear Kills
"It would seem that in societies where the effects of a curse are accepted as common knowledge,
there is no question that the spear of thought can kill."
—*Mysteries of the Unexplained*

There is always an element of fear in superstitions: fear we will jinx our favored baseball team unless we wear our jersey inside-out; fear we will break our mother's back if we step on a crack; seven years bad luck for breaking that mirror.

It is fear that gives power to superstitions.

Our body doesn't know the difference between real fear caused by an actual physical threat and superstitious fear caused by faulty reasoning. This is why a black cat crossing our path can cause the same reaction from our body as facing a down an actual tiger; that is, if we believe in the power of the black cat to curse us.

One explanation for how fear and superstition kill, and hence how the mind-slayer can kill with a single word, with a single thought placed in their victim's mind, is based as much on physiology as it is on psychology.

When faced with a threat (real or imagined) our body increases its production of adrenaline (you know, that same glandular secretion that allowed that woman to lift the car off her trapped child). Simultaneously, the body reduces blood supply to organs that are not immediately needed for "flight-or-fight" (such as the digestive system). By constricting the small blood vessels in these "non-essential" parts of the body, the body can then reroute blood to vital areas and to the limbs needed for flight-or-fight.

Unfortunately, when the blood supply is reduced to "non-essential" areas, the oxygen the blood carries is also reduced. Thus, prolonged fear reduces the overall volume of blood circulating through the body. Less blood circulation equals reduced blood pressure. Reduced blood pressure, in turn, adversely affects those parts of the body responsible for maintaining blood circulation in the first place and this further reduces circulation, further reducing blood pressure—on and on—in a vicious downward spiral that, if left unchecked, kills!

How Superstitions Survive
"Best safety lies in fear."
—Shakespeare, *Hamlet*

No matter how many times you explain to some people that viruses cause colds, they still stubbornly cling to their superstitious fear that getting their heads wet somehow causes colds. Madison Avenue understands this and tailors every television commercial for cold medications to reinforce this superstition.

How many of us step a little more carefully on Friday the 13th? Yet who among us can point to the true origin of the superstition?

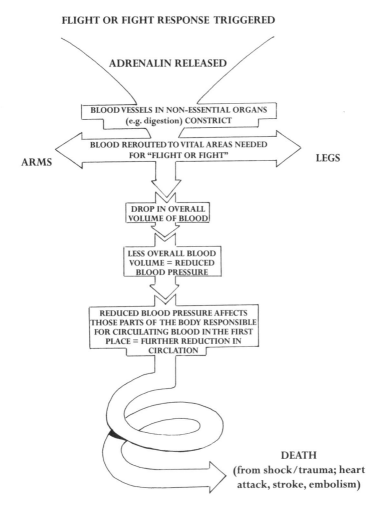

FLIGHT OR FIGHT RESPONSE TRIGGERED

ADRENALIN RELEASED

BLOOD VESSELS IN NON-ESSENTIAL ORGANS
(e.g. digestion) CONSTRICT

BLOOD REROUTED TO VITAL AREAS NEEDED
FOR "FLIGHT OR FIGHT"

ARMS

LEGS

DROP IN OVERALL
VOLUME OF BLOOD

LESS OVERALL BLOOD
VOLUME = REDUCED
BLOOD PRESSURE

REDUCED BLOOD PRESSURE AFFECTS
THOSE PARTS OF THE BODY RESPONSIBLE
FOR CIRCULATING BLOOD IN THE FIRST
PLACE = FURTHER REDUCTION IN
CIRCLATION

DEATH
(from shock / trauma; heart
attack, stroke, embolism)

What about Astrology? Modern astronomy teaches us that those same stars ancient peoples thought were close beside one another and all the same distance from the Earth—stars they then used to form their Zodiac "pictures" in the sky—are in reality billions of miles removed from one another and have no relation to one another whatsoever except for what primitive people without telescopes, and modern superstitious people without lives, give them.

Still, horoscopes continue to appear daily in every major newspaper.

Superstitions and rituals meant to invoke luck survive from generation to generation, passing from person to person like a virus, because of two factors.

First, sometimes our superstitious rituals actually do seem to work. This is called coincidental reinforcement. We walk across that same street a thousand times without incident, yet the time we survive almost getting run over we thank that rabbit's foot on our key-chain. Likewise, we buy a thousand lottery tickets and, so long as one of them is a winner, we will continue carrying our lucky four-leaf clover (the same talisman we had in our pocket for the other 999 losers!).

In other words, our rituals work some of the time, thus we keep using them.

Secondly, and more ominous, superstitions survive because we fear to trespass against them.

If we don't wear our lucky hat, our team will lose! If we don't scratch that lottery ticket with our lucky coin, we'll lose out on millions!

Mind-slayers root out any personal and/or cultural superstitions their potential victims consciously or subconsciously possess, knowing that within those superstitions is the key to controlling—even killing—those victims.

These strategies can range from something as simple as stealing a ballplayer's lucky glove prior to a play-off game to making a victim believe he has a terminal illness. Remember, all superstitions are based on fear. Remind yourself, fear kills!

This explains why superstitions so rarely die off, though those who trust in them all too often do!

Digging Up Dark Secrets
"I rather tell thee what is to be fear'd
Than what I fear."

—Shakespeare, *Julius Caesar*

A ruthless mind-slayer is one-half psychologist, one-half private investigator . . . and one-half undertaker. This makes up the 150 percent the mind-slayer needs to first dig up the dirt on his victim . . . and then bury him with it!

We all have secrets, if not out-and-out bloody secrets then at least skeletons in the closet whose dusty bones we'd rather not have rattled on *The Jerry Springer Show*.

These secrets can range from our own embarrassing lapses in judgement to secrets we are entrusted with by loved ones and friends. Mind-slayers are adept at digging up these secrets—the darker those secrets, the better.

Birth Secrets

At one time being born a bastard assured that your life was pretty much over before it began. While we no longer blame the children for being conceived outside marriage, an unwed mother is often still looked upon with disdain, and some individuals and families still go to great lengths to keep such things secret. Sometimes this requires sending the girl away to "visit relatives" in another state, then quietly putting the baby up for adoption.

This leads to another birth-related shock, finding out (or being made to think) you are adopted.

Unwanted pregnancy can also end in an abortion, which, while legal, isn't something the young woman (or her family) wants broadcast.

Body Flaws

We all have an image in our minds of "the perfect body." Unfortunately, none of us seem to have this body.

For teenagers, zits and freckles can undermine self-confidence. For the middle-aged, it's hair-loss or being fat—the latter often judged by others to be the result of lack of control or laziness.

Mind-slayers learn to spot and then exaggerate and exploit the smallest of body defects and deformities—real or imagined—both in the minds of the insecure individuals and/or in the minds of insensitive people around them.

Failure Secrets

Failure to achieve a dream of success makes many people frustrated and then bitter before their time.

Internally-motivated people torture themselves when they fail to meet their goals. (Of course, there is always a mind-slayer close by willing to lend them a cat-o-nine-tails!)

Externally-motivated people often feel they have failed to live up to others' expectations (e.g. parents, spouse, etc.). Mind-slayers get close to such people by promising to show them how to satisfy others.

Sex Secrets

From Hawthorne's *The Scarlet Letter* to the Clinton-Lewinsky scandal, sex has always been a hot potato (or in Clinton's case a cigar).

In addition to adultery (seen as a weakness in character), there are a host of other sex-related wounds people have into which the mind-slayer can twist a knife:

Unexpressed sexual fantasies can lead to secret guilt, humiliation (if revealed) and, when unearthed, can cause a person to be added to a mind-slayer's (black)mail route.

Feelings of impotence and inadequacy can lead people to go to extremes, from hiring a prostitute to jumping out of a plane to prove they're macho.

Since sex is often seen as the measure of a man's worth, feeling that we just don't measure up can undermine a man's self-confidence and lead to feelings of frustration, anger, even violence. The same thing happens when a woman thinks (or can be made to believe) that her actions or inactions have driven her lover into the arms of another.

Feelings of inadequacy often feed the fear of losing a lover, this in turn fuels suspicion and jealousy. Sex and jealousy go hand in hand. Making a person doubt his or her loved one's devotion drives a wedge between the two. The bigger the wedge, the more easily a mind-slayer can slip in.

Homophobia, fear of homosexuals and/or the fear of being (thought) gay can be a powerful slander against a person, either because others believe it, or because the person being targeted *fears* others will believe it. Another consideration is the effect of a loved one being (or even being thought) gay has on friends and family. Often when a gay person comes out of the closet, parents feel guilt ("Where did we go wrong?"), siblings fret it might be genetic and run in the family, and spouses think, "I drove them to this!" and begin to doubt their self-worth as wife or husband.

Even longtime friends have been known to abandon one another if one is thought to be gay, fearing people will think, "If your buddy is gay, you must be gay too!"

Mind-slayers know this and use such rumors to drive a wedge between friends and family, further undermining their victim's support network.

Molestation can also be used to both discredit a victim's credibility with others and even make the targeted people doubt themselves. Even false allegations of child molestation can ruin a career. The media are quick to plaster a person's name on the screen when he's accused of a heinous act (child molestation, rape), yet when's the last time you saw them run a follow-up story when the charges were dropped?

A second way molestation can be used is to convince your victim that he himself has been the victim of molestation as a child. Or, say a mind-slayer targets a rival businessman. Convincing that rival's teenage daughter to go to the authorities with memories she has suddenly recalled of being molested by her father as a child might be a good place to start.

Couldn't happen? You might want to study the 1988 Washington State case where, after attending a fundamentalist Bible camp which featured a "cult expert" lecturing on how prevalent "Satanic ritual abuse'" was "even in good Christian families," two daughters (aged 18 and 22) became convinced they'd been the victims of child abuse years before. This "revelation" led to the breakup of their family and the subsequent imprisonment of their father. (This case will be explored in more depth later in this chapter.)

Crime Secrets

From those paper clips we stick in our pocket as we're leaving work to our son's shoplifting problem, there is always a friendly mind-slayer giving us a conspiratory wink, willing to help us smooth things over or sweep it under the rug.

What they never tell you is that trying to cover such things up usually turns out to be twice as much trouble as the actual crime itself.

Illness Secrets

Sometimes illness is seen as a weakness on the part of the sick person. Other times illness is seen as something the person brought on himself (for example through drug abuse or lifestyle). When illness is combined with a sexual element, it is doubly useful to the mind-slayer. For example, AIDS is seen by some as God's punishment for a wicked lifestyle, or some other STD is your punishment for committing adultery.

The first step in crooked faith-healing is convincing the person they actually have an illness.

The only thing better than dealing in physical faith healing is tampering with mental illness, since the mind-slayer doesn't even have to produce any physical evidence (unlike psychic surgeons who have to at least palm some bloody chicken organs in order to remain convincing!).

The next best thing to making a foe doubt his own sanity, is making those around him doubt it for him. A classic cutting-at-the-edges ploy using this strategy was played out during the 1972 presidential campaign when presidential hopeful George McGovern's running mate, Senator Thomas Eagleton, resigned from the ticket after someone leaked to the media the fact that Eagleton had been hospitalized three times for treatment of emotional exhaustion and depression.

Whatever Eagleton's actual qualifications, the assumptions about his mental dependability made him a political liability, and effectively sank McGovern's campaign.

Death Secrets

We all dread the day that Ol' Grey Mower decides to knock on our door. Mind-slayers wrapped in the robes of religion count on this, selling us salvation from damnation.

Death always leaves unresolved feelings, what thanatologists call lack of closure. These unresolved feelings open the way for mind-slayers (psychics, cult leaders, etc.) to get their foot in the funeral home door. Feelings of responsibility and guilt (justified or not) over the death of another is a powerful motivator. Recall Yoshitsune's devious kyonin-no-jutsu plot against his evil brother.

The suicide of a loved one always leaves behind guilt in the survivors (i.e. "I should have seen the signs . . .") and mind-slayers are quick to exploit this guilt. Where guilt doesn't occur naturally, mind-slayers create it.

If their intended victim doesn't have any true dark secrets, it is necessary for mind-slayers to create them, or, resort to cutting at the edges by unearthing the dark secrets of the victim's friends and relatives.

Thus the mind-slayer patiently looks for weaknesses, digs up the victim's dark secrets, and collects the ammunition the mind-slayer all too often convinces the victim to aim at his own head!

The One-Eyed Snake

"Tricks well-mastered are called techniques.
Techniques half learned are merely tricks."
—Ralf Dean Omar, *Death on Your Doorstep*

Remember: Reputation often spills less blood. Thus shinobi ninja, like other secretive societies throughout history, intentionally drew around themselves an impenetrable shadow-cloak of mystery designed to dissuade casual interest and discourage deliberate assault. Outsiders were encouraged to believe the ninja were descended from the mysterious tengu demons and therefore possessed magical powers.

While we may never know whether the shinobi ninja truly possessed some sort of psychic ability, we do know that the shinobi used a strategy known as The One-Eyed Snake. This strategy was comprised of tactics and techniques intended to give outsiders the illusion they possessed true magical powers, in particular, the power to strike down a foe from afar and/or with a single touch without so much as a mark left on the victim.

Belief in this dreaded "death touch" (dim-mak) was first promoted by the moshuh nanren "ninja" of China.[5] The original art of dim-mak killed by interrupting the flow of a victim's chi (the body's vital energy). When using dim-mak, moshuh nanren targeted the victim's most vulnerable body spots during that victim's most vulnerable time of the day.

One-Eyed Snake techniques, on the other hand, only pretended to be true dim-mak. To accomplish this, ninja used poisons, specialized unarmed blows, and specially designed weapons, all of which left no marks on the victim's body.

For example, an assassin could place poison on his fingertips that, when coming into contact with the victim's skin, would seep into the victim's bloodstream, causing the victim to become ill and die in minutes, hours, or days, thus simulating a true death's touch. Other poisons were neurotoxic, paralyzing the nervous system like cobra venom, stopping the victim's heart within seconds.

The uses of such One-Eyed Snake poisons were many. For example, a ninja could secretly make a high-ranking official ill with poison, opening the way for a second ninja (posing as a healer or astrologer) to worm his way into the sick person's confidence by administering a miracle cure.

A variation on this miracle-cure ploy involved secretly poisoning a counselor of the emperor and then having a ninja spy posing as an astrologer accurately predict to the day, even to the hour or minute, when the counselor would die. When the specially timed poison did its job and the counselor dropped dead as predicted, the astrologer would instantly become an invaluable addition and trusted advisor to the emperor.

One of the most inventive One-Eyed Snake techniques, taken from the moshuh nanren, involved breeding silk worms that were fed poison so that the silk they spun was poisonous. Finely woven silk robes would then be presented as gifts to enemies.

Other One-Eyed Snake ploys included suffocating victims, cutting a victim's throat from the inside (by shoving a hook-ended blade through their mouths), and skewering into an enemy's brain with ice-pick weapons (through the nose or ear). Once, a ninja assassin succeeded in killing a hard-to-reach enemy by hiding for days under the man's toilet and then skewering up through the man's anus when the unsuspecting man sat on the crapper, killing the man without leaving a mark!

Still today, unscrupulous mind-slayers plying the faith-healers trade pretend to possess magical healing powers by using some of the same techniques developed by ancient ninja.

For example, faith-healers can secretly place healing anesthetic salves on their hands that, when touching a patient, makes the patient "feel" the healing.

More insidious still, an unscrupulous mind-slayer "priest" can secretly administer a psychosis-inducing drug to an unsuspecting cult member, then in full view of other cult members, perform an exorcism, curing the patient through merely the laying on of hands—hands soaked in the antidote, of course.

Wily shamans eat special herbs that are activated by the digestive juices in their stomachs to create a "hypnotic" vapor. A discrete belch then allows the shaman to exhale this "healing breath" onto the patient's face, making the patient woozy and thus more susceptible to suggestion.

Crafty hypnotists use similar ploys.

While the variations of the One-Eyed Snake are infinite, the purpose of the One-Eyed Snake strategy is always the same: to increase the superstition and fear others have of the mind-slayer whether in his guise as healer, astrologer, cult-leader, or assassin.

HYPNOTISM

"I' the name of something holy, sir, why stand you
In this strange stare?"
—Shakespeare, *The Tempest*

From ancient shamans and temple oracles, down to modern-day psychotherapists, ethical healers of the mind and unethical mind-slayers have used hypnosis.

According to one source, hypnosis in the West was derived from the practices of Asian shamans brought West by Jesuit missionaries.[6] However, ancient Celtic priests already claimed to possess a skill called "glamour" which meant to dazzle another's mind, often with only words.

The man credited with discovering hypnosis in the West is Marquis DePuysegur, a disciple of Dr. Franz Mesmer (1733-1851). From his studies of primitive shamanistic trances, Mesmer developed "animal magnetism," an early form of hypnotism. DePuysegur carried on Mesmer's research and during one session he observed one of his patients entering a trance-like state of true hypnotism.

By the mid-1800s, DePuysegur's hypnotism (a.k.a. "magnetic sleep") was being used to relieve patients' pain during operations in London. After observing patients' reactions while in magnetic sleep Sigmund Freud formulated his theory of the unconscious mind.

In 1852, researcher James Braid coined the term "hypnosis." Since then, hypnotism has been used to heal and to entertain. Hypnotism has also been used by mind-slayers for darker purposes.

What is Hypnotism?

Whether you know it or not, you've been in a hypnotic state literally thousands of times. Anytime you've been caught daydreaming or being absent-minded, you've been under a form of hypnosis.

Ninety percent of people can be deliberately hypnotized to some degree and of that number, fully 10 percent are highly suggestible and thus susceptible to being placed in deep levels of trance.

How does hypnotism work? We still don't know. We do know, however, that effective hypnotism depends on the power of suggestion.

The term absent-minded is appropriate since during hypnosis our usual controlling conscious "higher" mind is temporarily absent or asleep, while our "lower" subconscious "shadow mind" (responsible for emotion and motor control) is still awake.

Under hypnosis, our brains go to sleep while our lower brains, accustomed to being given commands by our higher brains, continue to take orders from the hypnotist. Thus, under hypnosis, this lower brain simply substitutes the outside commands of the hypnotist for the commands of its sleeping higher brain.

Three things make this hypnosis possible:

First, the subject's focus is narrowed to the point to where only a single source of information is coming into the subject's brain—information controlled by the hypnotist. The hypnotist then literally defines reality for the victim's subconscious mind.

Second, it is important the subject believe in the process of hypnosis and in the hypnotist.

Finally, for hypnotism to be successful the subject must be willing to suspend logic and temporarily accept distortions in cause and effect, and in his perception of time and space.

For example, a hypnotized subject can be given post-hypnotic suggestion to forget the number seven. When awakened from the trance and asked "What is three plus four?," the subject readily answers either "six" or "eight." Asked how many fingers he has, the subject correctly responds "10" and often seems unbothered by the fact he has an "extra" digit when asked to count his fingers.

Any time such discrepancies in logic appear, hypnotized subjects either attempt to rationalize them away or simply ignore them. This is known as trance logic and is often seen in cults where members go to great extremes to rationalize the bizarre and often contradictory actions of their leaders.

Putting Them Under

All hypnosis techniques first relax the body and then narrow the mind's focus, making the hypnotic subject oblivious to external stimulation, except for the voice of the hypnotist.

Hypnotic Strategies

There are three main approaches used to induce a hypnotic state:

- Single-point focus captures and holds the subject's attention on a single object (e.g. light, a swinging pendulum, a metronome, or a hypnotic coin);
- The command approach gives the subject direct instructions and works especially well where the hypnotist is seen as an authority figure; and
- The imagery approach uses analogies, symbols, and metaphors to separate the subject from his external environment. This approach is effective for use with those patients who resist the command approach.

Imagery approach induction allows the mind-slayer to craft commands designed especially to capture and hold the attention of the subject through use of his favored speech style. Tell watchers: "Picture in your mind . . ."; listeners: "Listen to the sound of my words . . ."; touchers: "Feel the soft breeze on your face, smell the flowers . . ."

The imagery approach is effective because it is difficult for a person to resist suggestions he does not consciously know he is receiving, that is, when the suggestion is disguised in symbolism that only the subconscious mind registers. This subliminal approach is favored by the unscrupulous—con men, cult leaders, and Madison Avenue.

How a subject views the hypnotist determines which of these hypnosis strategies will work best. Once the mind-slayer establishes himself as an authority figure, the command approach—direct repetitious orders used in connection with single-point focus—works best.

If the subject is on an informal or personal basis with the hypnotist (where subject and hypnotist are seen as equals), the imagery approach, augmented with single-point focus, works best.

The Power of Voice

The most important aspect of any hypnotic induction is the voice of the hypnotist.

The human voice alone can produce a hypnotic state because the pre-verbal "lower" brain remains in awe of "higher" brain's verbal ability.

Speech-Induced Trance

Before beginning, determine the subject's "type"—watcher, listener, or toucher—and mirror it when giving suggestions.

When inducing a hypnotic state by speaking:

* Avoid interruption in the flow of your words;
* Speak in short separate sentences tied together with "and";
* Speak in a rhythmic monotone "singsong" as pleasantly as possible, stretching out soothing and relaxing words: "looose . . . sleeepy . . . deeeply."

Types of Hypnotic Suggestions

The kinds of hypnotic suggestions given vary with their intended goals.

* *Relaxation suggestions* are designed to place the subject into a state more receptive to additional, more complex, suggestion.
* *Trance-deepening suggestions* take the subject to deeper levels of trance, opening him to deeper conditioning.
* *Imagery-building suggestions* reinforce the trance state with pictures of reality drawn by the hypnotist.
* *Direct command suggestions* order the subjects to do specific things, such as change his behavior.
* *Post-hypnotic suggestions* are orders given to the subjects that he carries out after being awakened from the actual trance. Mind-slayers refer to post-hypnotic suggestions as "time bombs."

Giving Hypnotic Commands

When giving hypnosis commands, follow these guidelines:

* Break complex goals into simple, more manageable ones. Use small steps to accomplish one goal at a time;
* Keep suggestions simple and concise, believable and desirable;
* Use positive words wrapped in clear and appropriate imagery;
* Repeat suggestions in order to reinforce them;
* Use synonyms as much as possible (the same words repeated over and over lose meaning);
* Avoid vague time periods such as "soon" or "in the future." Instead, give

definite time suggestions: "When I snap my fingers" or "Upon awakening." And, most importantly,

* Always include a post-hypnotic suggestion, for example a "trigger-
  word" that produces instant re-hypnosis any time the subject hears it.

Ninja Use of Hypnosis

Shinobi called hypnosis *yugen-shin*, "mysterious mind," and saw it as a
valuable tool for helping them accomplish their missions. Self-hypnosis was
taught to ninja students to improve their control over self, and hypnosis was
taught them so they could overshadow their foes.

Despite their bloodthirsty reputation, ninja preferred non-violent
means to an end. Hypnotism helped them accomplish this ideal. And, when
violence was unavoidable, ninja used hypnosis to strengthen their own
resolve, while undermining the resolve of foes.

Ninja use of hypnosis helped foster the belief—and fear—that all ninja
possessed the power to overshadow the minds of others. Hypnotism also
aided in the ninjas' miraculous vanishing acts after completing a mission.
Often a post-hypnotic suggestion left victims with the illusion that ninja possessed true magical powers (a là the One-Eyed Snake).

Self-Hypnosis

Self-hypnosis allowed these knights of darkness to relax themselves
physically and calm themselves mentally in preparation for dangerous missions. Ninja trainees were each given a post-hypnotic mantra-like trigger
word that when spoken aloud (or even thought of) in times of stress, fear, or
pain triggered their flight-or-fight adrenaline response.

Self-hypnosis was also used to enhance an agent's mental concentration, for
example, enhancing the memory of a ninja entrusted with a special message.

Often such carriers—whether ninja operatives or unwitting draftees—
would be given messages they were not consciously aware they were carrying until another agent at a prearranged rendezvous spoke a code word triggering a post-hypnotic suggestion to remember the information. On the flip-
side, agents could be given a hypnotic trigger-word to make them forget
information they carried if captured.

Of course, hypnosis was also used by ninja to manipulate foes.

Basic Hypnosis Exercise

To place another person in a light hypnotic trance, begin by having him sit back or lay down in a quiet, comfortable place. After guiding the subject for a few minutes of slow, deep breathing, instruct the subject as follows:

"Take a deep breath and remember that feeling you feel right before waking up after a really good night's sleep, when you feel yourself half-awake, half-asleep, oh, so comfortable and warm that you just want to lay there, relaxed, barely touching the bed, floating on a warm cushion of air, one part of you wanting to move, the other savoring the warm, relaxing, comfortable sensation of floating on a warm bed of clouds . . . so you reward yourself, resting relaxed, warm and comfortable, allowing your body to float, allowing your mind to drift comfortably from thought to thought . . ."

Do not rush your relaxation of the subject. The more relaxed your subject becomes, the deeper his hypnotic trance. Having relaxed your subject into a light hypnotic trance, gently draw his focus to the specific subject and/or suggestions you want to work on.

(Note: A light hypnotic trance state is actually better for learning suggestions than a deep trance.)

WAY OF THE WORD WIZARDS (JUMON-NO-JUTSU)

"Good words are better than bad strokes."
—Shakespeare, *Julius Caesar*

Ninja word wizards mastered the art of stabbing manipulative images, thoughts, and emotions into the minds of their enemies.

To craft these "mind-daggers," ninja called upon their understanding of jujushin, kyonin-no-jutsu, and the insight given them from studying shadow language. Ninja call this kiai-shin-jutsu, literally "shouting into the mind."

Words as Weapons

"Many have fallen by the sword, but not as many as by the tongue."
—Aprocrypha Sirach 28:18

Samurai Lord Asano of the 47 ronin fame was killed by a single word when he allowed himself to be angered by a word specially chosen by his rival to incite him into drawing his sword in the presence of the shogun. Like Asano, many of us are chained to "word slavery," and easily manipulated by the words we hear:

- Words that move us to tears;
- Words that shock and anger us;
- Words that can lull a baby to sleep;
- Words that can lull adults into a false sense of security;
- Words that can convince us to buy things we don't need and to buy into ideas we'd be better off without;
- Words that can heighten our awareness; and
- Words that can hypnotize us.

Mantra

Poetry of the 18th century Romantic Movement was specifically arranged to create a trance-like state when read correctly. Many religious chants and hymns are also designed to draw listeners into a hypnosis-like state, making them more susceptible to the underlying message.

Recall that our voices alone have the power to put another person (or ourselves) into a hypnotic trance. Ancient peoples respected and feared the power of words. Thus we have tales of heroes going in search of magic words that would grant them great power: "Abracadabra," "Open Sesame," or "Aum."

Some of these mysterious sounds and words were used to accomplish magic, others to freeze an enemy in his tracks. *The Kama Sutra* speaks of magical verses that have the power of "fascination" and makes reference to them appearing in ancient Indian texts such as the Indian *Anunga Runga* (*Kamaledhiplava*).

Down through the ages, many "words to conjure by" were sacred or forbidden. In India, these sacred sounds are known as mantra.

Yogi practitioners maintain that reciting these mantra can grant chanters all kinds of magical abilities. As a result, mantra formulas are found throughout the Far East, in the religions of Hinduism, Tibetan Lamanism, and Buddhism.

One theory claims that mantra are the original sounds made by primitive man to express basic emotions (fear, surprise, love, etc.) and that accounts for why mantra are recognized by the more primitive parts of our brains. Mantra vibrations act as codes that stimulate the brain on a subconscious level, in effect, acting like a TV remote control, changing our moods and energy levels.

Mind-slayers know the potential of the spoken word and use specially chosen words and phrases that put us under their spell before we know it.

The Art of Agreement

If you can get a person to say "yes" to a little point, he is more likely to say "yes" to a big point. In order to persuade others, mind-slayers first listen to them.

By listening to others—listening to their desires, their version of reality, letting them blow off steam and get it off their chests, you allow them to exhaust themselves. By listening to the other person's point of view we also see their best argument before they see ours.

Getting in Synch

When countering a person's argument, don't get personal. Attack the position rather than the person. Require him to defend his position, produce evidence, verify facts and explain his reasoning.

Since we tend to cooperate with people we like, those with whom we share common interests, once you determine his position and the direction his argument is taking, place yourself in synch with him by finding common ground and points of common interest.

Beginning a conversation, use wide, open and friendly arm gestures designed to grab the listener's attention. From these large gestures, gradually move inward, into smaller, more intimate hand gestures that gradually draw all the listener's focus onto you.

Pay attention to what others say as well as how they say it.

Watch the body language of the person you are trying to persuade (how he sits, moves, rate of breathing, gestures) then imitate his actions and attitudes.

Agreeing without Agreeing

No matter how different another person's argument is, the mind-slayer agrees with them, or at least appears to.

Using phrases like "I see your point," "I agree 100 percent," and "It would be hard to argue with that," mind-slayers effectively diffuse others' arguments and purposely drive a wedge between the person and his argument.

To accomplish this, first determine whether the person is trying to prove his point or trying to prove himself. In other words, does he really believe his point is worth arguing for and his position worth defending, or is he simply saying "Hey, look at me. I'm smart!"?

If the latter, assure him that he is, indeed, smart and valuable, that it's his *position* that's wrong. Acknowledge his concerns as valid and, most important, stroke his ego. You can recognize another's need to feel important and accepted without actually agreeing with him.

Make the person choose between promoting himself or promoting his argument. Make him choose between accepting your compliments or supporting his position. For example, tell him, "You're obviously an intelligent person, someone must have purposely given you incorrect facts."

Remember: Mirroring tells people you're just like them. Once adept at reflecting the other person, you can take control of the communication, adjusting the pace, tone, and direction of the conversation, gently guiding the conversation where you want it to go, leading the person into agreement with you.

To paraphrase Tu Mu, show him a way to safely withdraw from the conversation by creating in his mind an alternative to losing. Thus, when trying to bring a person into agreement with you, always leave him a face-saving way out of a disagreement, a way of honorably abandoning his position.

Two points work in the mind-slayer's favor when attempting to do this: the human need for personal consistency and our desire for social acceptance.

Personal Consistency

We all try to justify our earlier behaviors. Thus, when the mind-slayer points out that something we're doing or saying today contradicts yesterday's actions and opinions, we may go to great lengths to justify our actions.

Mind-slayers pay close attention to any inconsistencies in the other person's narrative, including contradictions between his stated goal and any effort (or lack of) he makes toward accomplishing his goal. Mind-slayers are quick to point out personal contradictions and inconsistencies in the argument of the person they are trying to persuade. They will either offer him a way to mend his inconsistencies (perhaps by showing him how your proposed course of action, your product, etc., helps him meet his goals), or else using his contradictions to further undermine his credibility.

Social Acceptance

We all care what other people think about us, especially people we look up to. Thus, the deep-seated sense of duty we feel toward authority figures (and institutions) can be invoked by mind-slayers in arguments with references to tribal totems, fallen heroes, and authority figures we admire and seek blessings from. Mind-slayers never tire of reminding us of our obligations.

(Note: Duty is a debt you owe yourself. Some call it honor. An obligation, on the other hand, is what other people try to tell you your duty is.)

The Craft of Lying
"To lapse in fullness
Is sorer than to lie for need, and falsehood
Is worse in kings than beggers."
—Shakespeare, *Cymbeline*

According to Dr. Robert D. Hare, psychopaths have a natural talent for lying, deceiving, and manipulation.[7] Lying may be a natural talent for psychopaths, but the rest of us have to practice! It has been speculated that lying may be a survival skill determined by genetics to save your lives. Of course, getting caught lying can also get you killed!

Despite that fact, a recent study determined that 91 percent of Americans lie regularly. Twenty percent admit they can't get through the day without telling a few premeditated "white" lies.[8]

More ominous still, people seem endlessly capable of justifying their lying—whether lying about their bowling score or about flying cocaine in from Central America in defense of God and country.

How to Spot a Liar
"There are three kinds of lies: lies, damn lies, and statistics."
—Benjamin Disraeli

For mind-slayers, becoming adept at unraveling a foe's wicked web of deceit is as important as learning to effectively weave their own.

Down through the ages, various techniques have been devised for testing truthfulness. Ancient Chinese placed rice powder in the mouths of suspected liars. The nervous liar's mouth would already be dry, thus a guilty person would be unable to speak. As dubious as some ancient lie-detection methods were, the accuracy of modern electronic lie-detection equipment is equally debatable. In the final analysis, even modern lie-detection equipment only does what we can learn to do with our eyes and ears, and through mastery of shadow language.

To trip up a liar, listen for verbal inconsistencies in his story, slips of his tongue, and other verbal clues. To do this, first slow down a fast-talking speaker so as not to allow his lies to get buried in all the bullshit he is shoveling your way. Remember to listen to *how* something is said in addition to *what* is said. Often what *isn't* said reveals the most.

Leakage

Look and listen for "leakage" tells at the end of a person's sentences and at the end of conversations. Leakage includes such things as changes in voice pitch, changes in breathing (deeper or shallower), inconsistencies in facts, and slips of the tongue, especially those that appear at the end of a conversation.

Also look for emotional leakage beneath the words. Disguising words is easy, disguising emotions difficult. Fleeting facial expressions often reveal genuine underlying emotion.

On the other hand, strong shows of emotion (anger, feigned indignation) may be a defensive strategy designed to divert attention from a lie.

In addition to verbal clues, remember to look for revealing body language tells a lying person is consciously unaware of, such as compulsive swallowing, nervous gestures, the initial nod a speaker unconsciously gives just before saying "no," and the almost imperceptible shrug coming right before he agrees with you (a sign the speaker is uncertain and has second thoughts).

Picking Up "Vibes"

Often we experience a vague feeling of unease, of "bad vibes," when listening to someone. This is because we subconsciously perceive lying "tells," words that don't match body language, warning us that we are being lied to.

To illustrate how important it is to match body language to words, try this experiment the next time a friend asks you a question: Nod "yes," but say "no." Watch the confusion on his face as his brain tries to reconcile two contradictory messages.

When talking to someone of questionable truthfulness, ask three "control" questions: a question you *know* the person knows the answer to, a question the person *might* know the answer to, and a question you know the person *doesn't* know the answer to. As the person responds, watch for the speaker's tells. Spotting tells in response to these different questions provides clues to his truthfulness. You can also use his answers to help you determine whether he is a watcher, listener, or toucher.

If you get a vibe someone is lying to you, he probably is and you are picking up on it on a subconscious level. Trust your "gut-feelings." Your "gut" evolved a few million years before your over-rationalizing brain.

Lying by Gender

Lying techniques vary by gender. In general, men make lies of commission (adding information), woman make lies of omission (leaving out important details).

When talking to a man, keep track of what he says, noting any inconsistencies, returning to contradictions and points needing clarifying at the end of his speaking.

When talking to a woman, pay attention to what she doesn't say. Look for gaps in the continuity of her narrative.

Rule of thumb: Men lean toward you when lying, women lean away.

The Power of Suggestion

Mind-slayers never give orders; they make suggestions. Sometimes these suggestions are direct, even blunt. At other times, circumstances and the sensibility of their victims require mind-slayers to make less direct—but nevertheless effective—suggestions.

When a less direct attack is called for, mind-slayers employ a variety of symbols, gestures, and word-play tactics that allow them to influence their victims on a subliminal level.

Subliminal Suggestion

Toward the end of the 1950s there was a public panic when it was revealed that advertisers were trying to influence buyer behavior on a subconscious level by planting hidden messages in advertisements and in movies. These messages were called "subliminal suggestions" (from the Latin sub-limen, meaning "below consciousness").

The idea of using subliminal messages is hardly new.

Third century Indian Yoga master Pantanjali taught that thoughts (caused by seeing a symbol, hearing a word, etc.) or any physical act (such as gestures made by another) leave behind impressions (*samskara*) that subtly (subliminally) influence a person's future thought and actions.

Subliminal suggestion works in two ways: first by creating an association of one thing with another in a viewer or listener's mind and, second, by taking advantage of preconceived connections the person has.

To accomplish this, mind-slayers employ a host of words-ploys, evocative symbols, and gestures targeting these subliminal connections.

Madison Avenue fully understands the value of subliminal suggestion. That's why the Pillsbury Doughboy is modeled after a fetus (baking and giving birth being closely related in women's minds) and why Joe Camel's nose is modeled after male genitalia (associating smoking with "manly" virility).

Subliminal suggestion works best when attacking the viewer or listener on an emotional level rather than on a higher reasoning level. Evoking an emotional response via subliminal suggestion is called subception.

The carriers of these subliminal messages can employ any number of words, symbols, or gestures purposely designed to penetrate into a person's mind castle without his normal conscious "gatekeeper" recognizing them as dangerous or superfluous, and thus turning them away.

Psychology pioneer B.F. Skinner once proved how his Behaviorism theory of psychology could be used to subliminally affect noted psychoanalyst Erich Fromm, who had disputed Skinner's findings that showed just how easily human behavior could be shaped or manipulated.

Attending a lecture Fromm was giving, Skinner passed a note to a friend, "Watch Fromm's left hand. I'm going to shape a chopping motion."

From then on, every time Fromm raised his left hand to emphasize a point, Skinner looked directly at him with a steady gaze. When Fromm lowered his hand, Skinner nodded and smiled. Within five minutes, Fromm was chopping the air so vigorously that his wristwatch kept slipping over his hand![9]

Skinner's manipulation worked because, on a subconscious level, Fromm craved Skinner's approval. Thus, Skinner's subliminal gestures were able to influence Fromm's actions.

Words are the most oft used tool in the mind-slayer's subliminal bag of tricks. Correctly crafting subliminal suggestions requires distinguishing between neutral words and emotional words.

For example, "coffee" is a neutral, unambiguous word carrying only one meaning. The word coffee does not evoke an emotional response in us. A word like "death," on the other hand, evokes a host of emotional reactions (unease, fear, excitement).

Emotional words have more impact because we "file" them in more than one place in our brains. Deliberately using emotional words therefore allows the mind-slayer to penetrate more of our brain than using "neutral" words would.

Word Play

We all enjoy wordplay. All our jokes are based on a slip of the tongue, misunderstood or mispronounced words, or on words with double meaning.

Mind-slayers often use wordplay to place subliminal suggestions in their victims' mind. This wordplay includes the manipulation of sentence structure (syntax), the Theory of Liaison, the use of homophones.

The Theory of Liaison

Subliminal suggestions can be placed into another's mind by using words that, while by themselves are innocent, when spoken together with another innocent word create a third "subliminal" word-image.

For example, while the words "loose" and "exchange" have neutral meanings in and of themselves, when pronounced together, the phonetic ending of "loose" joins with phonetic beginning of "exchange" to form "sex." Likewise, the neutral juxtaposed words choose-examples and views-expected also form the liaison "sex."

In practical application, an unscrupulous seducer can liberally seed their friendly proposal with liaison words that subliminally plant the idea-image of "sex" in their listener's mind.

Likewise, using liaison, politicians and cult leaders preach to us of our "common need" (common need = "money").

The advent of computers allows for the creation of tens of thousands of liaison combinations. Thus during the course of a 30-second commercial, or a 30-minute lecture, mind-slayers using liaison can implant any number of subliminal images in their audience's collective mind.

Homophones

Words that sound like other words can also affect us on a subliminal level. You see a beautiful woman. Do you want to meet her or *meat* her? Here is the basis for so much of our humor.

Here is also the key to how mind-slayers use wordplay to confuse and control us.

Mind-slayers also often use "pairing," associating one word with another, exploiting already perceived connections in people's minds. Homophones work perfectly for this.

For example, during Desert Storm, President George Bush was advised by his political and military strategists to deliberately pronounce Saddam Hussein's name as "Sodom," as opposed to the more proper "Sah-*damn*." This was done in order to provoke the connection in Western minds with wicked Sodom(y) and Gomorrah.

When subtlety is called for, being able to present ideas to others as suggestions—especially subliminal suggestions—is a vital skill for the mind-slayer.

More important still, for self-defense, we must also learn to recognize any subliminal messages—intentional or unintentional—that could be used to overpower ourselves and our loved ones.

MASTERMINDS AND BLACK MAGICIANS

No fictional mind-slayer is more devious than the title character in *King Richard III*. Yet Shakespeare based his play on the real Richard (1452-1485) who schemed and murdered his way to the throne.

Fictional depictions of manipulating ninja mind-slayers are hardly less flattering. But although fiction is exciting, the ninja's ability to penetrate into the minds of others is well documented and no less fascinating. Surrounded by enemies, medieval shinobi mastered mind-control for self-defense and the elimination of foes.

Today, we would be naive to think there aren't still criminals, cult leaders, and tyrants that possess few qualms about using every mind-control secret in the book for ill, for thrill, and for personal gain.

Crimes of the Mind

"It should be understood that every country has its criminal element and that criminals the world over are an opportunistic lot with the predator's sense for sniffing out inherent weaknesses in situations and individuals. Where others see a natural disaster, the criminal mind sees an opportunity to plunder. Where honest folk see the terrible ravages of war, the criminal sees an opportunity to sell guns or set up a black market."

—Dr. Haha Lung[10]

Criminal mind-slayers range from confidence swindlers and sinister seducers to out-and-out killers, all of whom lurk in the corridors of the mind looking for victims.

These mind-stalkers are always on the alert for new and inventive ways to ensnare their prey.

For example, the Russian scientist known for his creation of a hi-tech "mind-control" machine that the U.S. government reportedly considered using against David Koresh at Waco, says he regularly gets visits from the Russian Mafia asking to use his device to get the edge on their business partners.

Smooth-talking criminals and con men always prefer bullshit to bullets.

The Confidence Man

"A good psychopath can play a concerto on anyone's heartstrings."
—Dr. Robert D. Hare[11]

By definition, all mind-slayers are "confidence men"—confident in their abilities to weasel their way into our confidence, confident all human beings have flaws that can be exploited, confidently wielding the manipulation skills necessary to undermine our confidence.

Beyond fictional depictions in *The Sting, The Flim-Flam Man*, and *The Grifters*, Eastern and Western history is filled with real silver-tongued, black-hearted rogues all too adept at leaving their victims red-faced. These real-life mind-slayers range from Russia's Rasputin to Utah's "Resurrection Man."

Today Alta, Utah, is a ski resort. But in 1873 it was a lawless mining town. In a kyonin-no-jutsu ploy worthy of any ninja mind-slayer, a stranger dressed all in black appeared in town one day announcing he possessed the power to resurrect the 100 gunmen buried in Alta's Boot Hill.

Fear sliced through the small mining town like a scythe.

Some of the miners wanted to hang the stranger. But finally the most superstitious miners passed the hat, collecting $2,500 to bribe the "Resurrection Man" into leaving Alta permanently.[12]

To show how little people change, 120 years later in Salem, Massachusetts, a similar rogue was convicted of swindling $500,000 from an heiress by convincing her he was a witch.[13]

Confidence men mix eloquent, pandering language and pleasing looks with captivating body language and mesmerizing mannerisms, dealing out offers too good to be true. To this, they add a dash of natural and/or practiced charisma with a liberal spicing of deliberate distraction and pressure ploys, creating an intoxicating mind stew that's sweet in the mouth but bitter in the belly.

Mind-slayers reason with you, wear you down with their incessant arguments, command, and, when necessary, threaten—anything to accomplish their agenda. These sinister students of human nature become adept at spotting innate weaknesses and dark secrets in others. They understand all our fears and foibles. They know that nine times out of 10, even when they take us for all we're worth, we won't go to the authorities for fear of looking foolish, or for fear of being arrested as a greedy accomplice in our own downfall.

They know all our dark secrets, or at least can make us believe they do.

In their informative study of the Japanese mafia, *Yakuza* authors David E. Kaplan and Alec Dubro relate how one enterprising gangster sent out thousands of letters to prominent Japanese reading simply: "I know what you did and I will reveal your secret to the world unless you send me money!"

Despite the fact no specific wrongdoing or actual secret was mentioned in the letters, despite the fact that no specific extortion amount was mentioned, the money was soon rolling in from those fearing someone had discovered their dark secret . . . whatever it was!

Mind-slayers make us prance to psychological tunes, step lively to patriotic marches, and dance religious jigs till Jesus comes home. Some of these rogues feign mental powers while others twist the legitimate tools of psychology and hypnotism to their dark purposes.

Black Hypnosis

"Hypnotism, and the act of depriving another person of choice or use of will, does constitute one of the most loathsome forms of black magic."

—Israel Regardie[14]

In the hands of ninja, hypnotism was a formidable weapon. Captured individuals were hypnotized and then released after being programmed with post-hypnotic suggestions designed to be triggered when the victim heard a specific code word whispered, was confronted by a specific sign or symbol, or even when he smelled a special blend of perfume.

When true hypnotism couldn't be done, ninja mind-slayers resorted to One-Eyed Snake strategies that mimicked real hypnotism. Many of these fake hypnosis techniques are still used by unscrupulous hypnotists today.

Hypnosis Dirty Tricks

"About a Svengali taking advantage of an unwilling Trilby: it can happen that an emotional, gullible person in need of mastermind-ing, may fall under the spell of a stronger, positive personality."

—Hans Holzer[15]

While clinical hypnosis is now a respected tool used by both the medical and psychiatric communities, the type of hypnotism the average person is familiar with is audience-participation stage hypnosis.

When it comes to using hypnosis, mind-slayers hedge their bets by not only studying the legitimate techniques of hypnosis used by doctors and psychologists, but also by studying the tricks of the trade of stage hypnotists. While most stage hypnotists are capable of inducing true hypnosis, there are some who use skullduggery rather than true hypnosis to accomplish their effects.

Stage hypnotists use their knowledge of body language and personality typing to spot the most susceptible subjects. They then use a combination of psychological and physical ploys to "put them under."

Spotting a Good Hypnosis Subject. The stage hypnotist's greatest skill is the ability to spot those people most likely to obey his commands without question. Stage hypnotists therefore select only the best subjects from a group of volunteers, those with a predisposition to obey. People don't volunteer unless they want to take part in the show. They avoid those volunteered by friends. The best subjects for hypnosis appear enthusiastic, cooperative, outgoing, and funny. They are natural hams.

Listeners (as opposed to watchers or touchers) make excellent hypnosis subjects since they pay special attention to words.

A quick test of subjects' ability to take commands: Have the group hold their arms straight out. Note those who respond immediately, without questioning looks on their faces. Eliminate those whose arms begin wavering after 30 seconds.

Psychological Hypnosis Tricks. With rare exceptions, the process of hypnosis requires at least a minimum of cooperation from the subject. In a clinical setting, it is important the patient agrees to be hypnotized.

On stage, not only do most subjects want to be hypnotized, but they are willing—to some extent—to play along with the hypnotist. Often, even if an individual is not truly hypnotized, if he sees others appearing to be hypnotized, he will play along with the crowd, even to the point of convincing himself he *is* truly hypnotized. For this reason, when a stage hypnotist chooses a group from the audience, you can bet at least one of them is a "shill," a confederate whose job it is to convince the other members of the group that the hypnotist actually has the power to hypnotize them.

The old saying among stage hypnotists is: "If you can hypnotize one, you can hypnotize 100." In other words, people tend to go along if they see someone else doing it.

Hypnotists also play on subjects' egos by assuring them that "the more intelligent you are, the better you respond to hypnosis."

Physical Hypnosis Tricks. Initially the hypnotist must get his foot in the door. If the hypnotist can convince the subject that he has the power of hypnosis, then the subject's skepticism will disappear and he will truly be drawn into a trance.

Unscrupulous mind-slayers have a variety of physical tricks they use to accomplish this.

One hypnotist rigged his subjects' chair to give a slight electrical shock, making anyone sitting in it "tingle" as soon as the hypnotist started "putting them under." This tingling sensation convinced the subject the hypnotist had "the gift." Other hypnotists give suggestions to their subjects that they will smell a certain odor (secretly sprayed in the air by the hypnotist). Others will be made to touch items coated with sugar and then touch their fingers to their mouth right before the hypnotist suggests they remember the taste of a birthday cake. Itching powder has been used to induce the suggestion of itching.

Hypnotists often keep a mint in their mouth, breathing this soothing vapor into the subject's face in order to relax them. Others spray a light vapor of ether, chloroform, or other calmative agent onto the victim in order to make the victim light-headed. To accomplish this the hypnotist hides a small squeeze-ball up his sleeve.

Modern hypnotists can flood the room with relaxing positive ions or with very low-frequency (VLF) waves specially tuned to make a victim more susceptible to the hypnotist's commands.

When all else fails, the hypnotist can bulldog a subject by pinching the back of the subject's head and/or squeezing the side of his neck to constrict the carotid arteries just below the Adam's apple. This cuts the blood-flow to the victim's brain. Even slight pressure can cause dizziness and loss of consciousness as the victim passes out into a "trance."

While a useful tool in the hands of ethical therapists, in the hands of unethical mind-slayers (con men, cult leaders, and rogue government elements) hypnotism can be a frightening tool.

Crime and Hypnosis

While the common belief is that you cannot make people under hypnosis do what they wouldn't normally do when not under hypnosis (e.g. commit crimes or immoral acts), mind-slayers know how to frame hypnotic and post-hypnotic suggestions so as to make their victims willing to participate in the unthinkable.

Thus, whereas an otherwise loyal servant would never consciously agree to betray his master, that same servant could be given the post-hypnotic suggestion: "You will open the (usually locked) widow in your master's bedroom so that your master can enjoy the night breeze." An agent could then take advantage of the open window to enter the residence. A variation of this ploy involves convincing the servant that a poison he is to give his master is really medicine.

Therefore, while it is universally agreed that no one under hypnosis can be forced to commit an act he knows is wrong, he can be tricked into committing an illegal or immoral act if the mind-slayer first convinces him it is right.

Numerous experiments have shown that, given the proper justification, hypnotized subjects can be made to steal, lie, and according to one experiment, even throw acid in another person's face.[16]

Critics claim that the hypnotized subjects still *know* it is only an experiment.

This leads to a logical question: Why couldn't a mind-slayer hypnotize a victim into believing an illegal or immoral action was "only an experiment" in order to convince the subject to commit questionable acts, up to and including murder?

A recent example of hypnosis being used to aid in the commission of a crime involves a Virginia man who was accused of sexually assaulting a man he had placed in a hypnotic trance at a stop-smoking clinic.[17] Another involved a bank robber in Reggio di Calabria, Italy, who hypnotized a bank cashier into giving him $4,000 during a hold-up.[18]

Murder by Hypnosis

In the 1950s, the possibility of hypnosis being used to commit crime was debated by legal experts after psychologists determined that an unscrupulous hypnotist who really wanted to use hypnosis to commit murder could almost certainly do it.[19] There are at least two documented cases in the United States of hypnosis being used as a murder tool, one successful, the second barely averted.

In 1894, a man confessed to having killed a girl while under a hypnotic spell. The hypnotized killer received a life sentence and his hypnotist was hanged.[20]

A second murder-by-hypnotism, also in 1894, was barely averted in time when the hypnotized victim "woke up" from the post-hypnotic suggestion he had been given to shove the target—the hypnotist's wife—into the Grand Canyon.

The hypnotist in this second case was Dr. Henry Meyer, who it was later discovered had left a string of corpses from New York to Chicago. Meyer had studied hypnotism in Leipzig, Germany, under one of the most celebrated mesmerists of the era, Professor Herbert Flint. By the time he got around to targeting his second wife, Meyer had reportedly murdered several people in order to collect on insurance policies, including his first wife.

In preparation for killing his second wife, Meyer hypnotized a plumber named Bretz to believe that Mrs. Meyer was in love with him so Bretz would run off with her to the Grand Canyon. Meyers had already given Bretz a post-hypnotic suggestion to push the woman into the Grand Canyon once they got there. The two lovers "eloped" and were actually standing at the edge of the Grand Canyon before Bretz shook off Meyer's spell.

The two returned to Chicago and reported the incident to the police, but a grand jury opted not to indict the good doctor. Meyer was set free, but was subsequently arrested for another murder.[21]

In the hands of devious and immoral mind-slayers, the potential for the misuse of hypnotism is obvious. It's not just the Rasputins and the Mansons we need to watch for, but the potential for the art to be systematically mis-used by cults, police, and rogue government elements.

There are documented cases of police using forced hypnosis to obtain confessions.[22] There are also documented instances of government attempts to use hypnosis for brainwashing.

The Cult Craft
"And thus I clothe my naked villainy with
odd old ends stolen forth of holy writ,
And seem I a saint, when most I play the Devil."
—Shakespeare, *King Richard III*

"Cult" is what the big religion calls the little religion, what the old reli-gion calls the new.

At one time or another, every new religion has been accused of being a cult. Christianity was originally branded a cult by Jewish authorities.

Modern sociologists and religious historians now avoid using the term "cult," which is inherently elitist, insulting, and implies that members of these groups are "mind-control victims."

Political correctness aside, many of these members *are* mind-control victims!

For every sincere religious leader in history there have always been nine morally bankrupt religious opportunists and extremists eager to prey on the spiritual needy.

More than three million Americans belong to more than a thousand separate groups that qualify as "cults." These cults come in religious, political, and secular varieties—from breakaway religious sects and mystical New Age schools, to motivational self-help organizations. These cults are not limited to any one age, gender, or race.

What qualifies each of these as a cult is the fact that, no matter what their outward teachings and trappings appear to be, their inner workings, ruthless recruiting methods, and heavy-handed indoctrination techniques vary little.

Three areas act as warning signs that a group—religious or secular, no matter how sincere their beliefs—have crossed the line to become a cult: their attitude (mind-set), their recruiting tactics, and their identity-stripping indoctrination methods.

Cult-Think

Cults and the people trapped in them don't think like the rest of us. Their "cult-think" allows them to pick and choose the parts of reality that suit them, that support their version of the universe, a universe easily identifiable since they are always at the center of it. Other important aspects of cult-think include:

Cults Claim a Monopoly on "The Truth"

For cults, there is only one locked box of "The Truth" to which only they possess the key.

Sometimes this key is a sacred book containing all "The Truth," past and to come. Other times, "The Truth" comes in the form of an all-seeing leader with a special pipeline to salvation.

Cult Views Are Not Open to Interpretation

Cults are intolerant of any challenge to their version of, and exclusive guardianship of, "The Truth." Cults view the world in simplistic terms: black and white, good or evil (as in the cult is good, the rest of the world is evil).

Cults Don't Tolerate Dissent

Cults discourage open discussion, punishing any member who dares question the cult's doctrine and leader(s), often assaulting and even killing outsiders who "blaspheme" against their leader, their sacred scriptures, or the group's collective identity.

Cults Move from Love to Menace

Cult messages begin with "love" but always end with a threat. Cult members approach potential recruits and potential financial contributors with "The Good News," and talk of "universal love and brotherhood." But the moment you reject (i.e. openly question) their message, their facade of "bliss" and "brotherhood" crumbles into frustration and their "message of love" quickly turns to veiled and not-so-veiled threats of what will happen to "non-believers" on the "Day of Judgement" when the cult takes power.

Cults Teach Separateness

Cults never tire of telling us (and themselves) how different they are from every such group that has come before. Cult members also never tire of reminding each other how different they are from "the infidels," often adopting outlandish dress and mannerisms to emphasize the point.

Cults Teach Dependence

Legitimate religious and self-help groups emphasize the empowerment of the individual.

Cults on the other hand make individuals totally dependent on them. To accomplish this, cults demand that recruits turn over any personal money they might have. In return, the cult will see to all their "needs." Without money, the individual becomes dependent on the cult for everything.

Another way a cult takes away an individual's independence is to take control of more and more of the recruit's time. This takes the form of holding the new member to a strict regimen of specific prayer times, bathing and eating rituals, and mandatory group studies, all designed to take away more of an individual's "free time"—emphasis on the word "free."

The Cult and the Leader Come First

Cults exist only to promote themselves and their agendas. Thus, the cult and it's leader(s) are always more important than any single member. Members are encouraged to sacrifice all their bothersome personal wants—friends, family, identity, and wallet—for the higher needs of the cult and its leader(s).

Cults Control

Cults are compulsive about control, managing every aspect of a member's life, and are committed to wiping out the last vestige of individuality.

Members are given strict standards of dress, deportment, and special greetings—salutes and recognition phrases to parrot when meeting other cult members.

Members are forced to adopt strict dietary rules. Abrupt and drastic changes in diet literally change brain and body chemistry, affecting mood and energy levels. This makes recruits less able to resist the cult's brainwashing.

It is possible to find people who hold extremist views that qualify as cult-think who actually belong to recognized religious and social organizations that are not cults per se. Mind-slayers are quick to spot and exploit these fanatics. The more extreme, unreasonable, and unbending a person's views, the easier it is to manipulate that person by simply adding fuel to the fire.

Cult Indoctrination

Change of diet, sleep deprivation, physical stress, and psychological strain can all work together to put a person into a receptive hypnotic state.[23] Cult mind-slayers use these tactics and more to break down recruits, making them more susceptible to indoctrination.

Indoctrination Ploys

Cult indoctrination strategies use physiological and psychological tactics.

Physiological tactics break a person down physically. This includes controlling members through isolation, making drastic changes in diet designed to induce physical weakness, and mandatory participation in various types of physical training (strenuous work, yoga-like exercises, mandatory prayer postures), all designed to produce hyperventilation, dizziness, and exhaustion.

After a hard days work filling the cult's purse, exhausted—hence more receptive—members are forced to attend mandatory classes and/or listen to long speeches by the cult leader.

Psychological ploys attack the recruit's former beliefs and self image. To accomplish this, cult mind-slayers cut recruits off from all outside sources of information, and use hypnosis and memory manipulation. In many ways, cult indoctrination resembles induction into army boot camp.

The major difference between boot camp training and cult indoctrination is that the aim of boot camp is to challenge the individual to go beyond previous self-limitations, to make the individual stronger, both physically and mentally. Cults, on the other hand, aim to weaken recruits, undermine any vestige of self-worth, and make recruits more susceptible to cult programming.

The Manufacture of Identity

"If you really want to change people, change their appearance."
—Margaret Thaler Singer[24]

Once initiated into the cult, recruits must discard their old names and appearances and adopt new identities provided by the cult. Cult recruits must wear extremes of dress (distinctive hats, robes) meant to further isolate them from non-members.

Memory Manipulation

Our memories are our identities. The further back our memories go, the more identity we have and the more rooted we feel. That's why cults go to great lengths to create fantastic cult histories stretching back into the distant past.

Our memories are not perfect records. They are instead reconstructions. Studies have shown that at least 25 percent of people are susceptible to having false memories implanted in their brains. In fact, memory researchers have successfully implanted false memories in people's minds, making subjects "remember" characters that never existed and events that never happened.[25]

Try this experiment: Read the following list of words to a friend: sugar, honey, cake, candy, icing, as long a list of synonyms of "sweet" you can think of. After waiting a few minutes, read the list back to your friend, asking him to identify which of the words you said before. While reading back the list, insert the word "sweet." Most people will say that "sweet" was one of the original words, a false memory, because all the words listed are associated with being sweet.

The easiest false memories to implant are at least mildly traumatic and are planted by a trusted or admired figure (e.g. relative, friend, or authority figure). Since true memories are richer in sensory details than false memories, mind-slayer hypnotists must add vivid imagery and sensory details to their suggestions especially designed to fit the victim's type (watcher, listener, toucher).

Cults can manipulate memory to convince recruits they've experienced visions or heard the voice of God. Sometimes cults dig up "memories" of a recruit's "past lives" (where, coincidentally, they belonged to the same cult). Other times, cults help recruits unlock "repressed memories" of spousal and/or parental abuse (a tactic for further alienating recruits from former friends and family).

Cults go out of their way to suppress any pleasant memories recruits cling to of their lives before the cult. Cults also suppress real memories of cult contradictions and abuse.

Some cults use a combination of hypnotism and drugs (narcohypnotism), which together are very effective for creating amnesia.[26]

Hidden Agendas

The major difference between military boot camp and cult indoctrination is that the boot camp agenda is overt and abrupt, while cults are covert and subtle.

Changing a person's thinking works best when the person is unaware he is being manipulated. Thus cults keep recruits unaware of the cult's hidden agenda until the recruit is completely ensnared. Objects in motion tend to stay in motion. Once in a cult, people tend to stay in.

Cult members programmed to believe that their leader and the cult's teachings are infallible, tend to blame themselves when something seems contradictory. They tell themselves that the contradictions must be a result of their misperception of the leader's actions, of their misinterpretation of "infallible" holy scripture. In for a penny, in for a pound. Cult members always find ways to rationalize away any contradictions in the cult's message or in the cult leader's behavior.

This kind of cult rationalization is the same kind shown by hypnotized subjects, such as the man who is given the hypnotic suggestion to forget the number seven and then must rationalize where he acquired an "extra" finger. Rather than openly question and leave when doubts arise, ensnared cult members actually redouble their efforts to be good followers, even to the point of dying with their leader rather than surviving and having to face the criticism of the outside world. Do the names Jonestown, Guyana, or Heaven's Gate ring a bell?

Conclusions

If you think you might be in a cult, you probably are!

For some, facing real world problems and making adult decisions every day is too daunting. It's easy to give in and allow someone else to do the worrying for a while. Mind-slayers know this and are all too eager to take our lives off our hands, offering us a nice, safe haven from the world—inside their cult.

Watching Big Brother

By 1590 Hideyoshi Toyotomi had succeeded where no other leader before him had, uniting the islands of Japan. Hideyoshi's rise to power—from thief, to spy-for-hire, to able general, and finally to dictator of Japan—was due to his ninja trained insight into the human mind.

Hideyoshi's reign was so successful because he was an accomplished ninja mind-slayer who masterfully used psychological plots and ploys to confuse potential enemies, and used propaganda to cower and control the masses.

Hideyoshi was not the first—and unfortunately not the last—ruthless government leader to use mind-manipulation to control citizens.

Throughout history, from the building of the Tower of Babel down to the babbling of present day politicians, government agencies and police have used mind-slayer psychology, propaganda, and brainwashing to control the very people they were intended to serve.

The Sixties

The 1960s were the heyday of mind-control experiments in the United States.

While rebellious youth experimented with a kaleidoscope of Eastern mysticism and psychedelic drugs to free their minds, shadowy government agencies (our own and, in at least one case, a foreign government) also experimented with psychotropic chemicals, experimental devices, and even "killer psychics," all in an effort to influence the minds of Americans.

According to firebrand Lyndon LaRouche, there was a concerted effort made by British Intelligence to "dumb down" the United States with drugs and rock music during the '60s. According to this scenario, many antiestablishment "hippie" leaders and rock stars were really unwitting stooges of the British Secret Service.

As outlandish as this tale might at first appear, it is a known fact that at least one '60s counterculture icon, Jerry Garcia of the band The Grateful Dead, took part in what was later found to be CIA-sponsored LSD experiments in the San Francisco bay area.

Likewise, it has been proposed that government-sponsored mind-control experiments that took place in the California prison system in the 1960s and '70s may be responsible for helping create such monsters as Charlie Manson and may have led (inadvertently?) to the 1980s "explosion" of serial killers:

"Victor Marchetti, author of *The CIA and the Cult of Intelligence*, confirmed . . . that the agency did indeed have a program of experimental mind control and that it used prisoners in American penal institutions as its subjects."[27]

For decades, including the '60s, the Central Intelligence Agency experimented with several mind-altering drugs, not the least of which was LSD. These included atropine (a poison); scopolamine (a depressant); sodium amytal and sodium pentathal (so-called truth serums); and aminazine (the Soviet sister to thorazine), all of which made subjects more "open" to programming.

But the CIA was not the only U.S. government agency to experiment with the minds of U.S. citizens:

- The U.S. Army admits to giving LSD to 2,000 subjects over an eight-year period in the '60s.
- Between 1954 and 1975, the Department of Health, Education and Welfare tested LSD on 2,500 prisoners, mental patients, and paid volunteers.
- The government also gave millions of dollars in grants to more than 30 university researchers for LSD testing on human subjects, primarily college students.[28]

Reportedly, several suicides and psychotic reactions occurred amongst those subjects who were given drugs such as LSD without their knowledge.[29] Beyond these documented admissions of abuse are accounts of government mind-control research ranging from the recently declassified to the outright bizarre: from UFO disinformation campaigns and attempts at mass subliminal suggestion, to "backwards-masking" on rock-n-roll records.

Three cases from the '60s illustrate better than all others the extent to which modern governments can go in the use and misuse of mind-manipulation.

The first deals with successful government mind-control techniques intended to turn an ordinary person into an unwitting government agent.

The second illustrates how those citizens with special skills can have their abilities callously perverted for questionable government gain.

The third is a cautionary tale from the '60s, warning that all of us are susceptible to mind-slayers targeting our need to belong and tempting us with promises of absolute power.

The Seduction of Candy Jones

In 1943, G.H. Estabrooks and E.P. Dutton published the book *Hypnotism,* which contained a chapter entitled "Hypnotism in Warfare: The Super Spy." Estabrooks and Dutton advanced the theory that hypnotism could be used to plant information so deeply in an agent's subconscious that it could not even be tortured out of him since the information would not be in the agent's conscious mind.

This idea, of using hypnosis to augment the abilities of agents, is nothing new.

As mentioned earlier, Japanese ninja and other groups (moshuh nanren, Hashishins, the Thuggee) successfully used hypnotized agents. Following World War II, with the rise of the Cold War, great strides were made in the black science of mind-manipulation.

All the bizarre theories, techniques, and fears of Cold War mind control came together in the case of Candy Jones.

During the '40s and '50s, Candy Jones was one of America's leading models. In a single month, she made the cover of 11 magazines and was featured in a smash Broadway play. By 1960, having fallen on hard times, Candy was approached by the CIA to act as a courier. She accepted and worked for the agency for the next 12 years.

Then, in 1972, after she began suffering emotional problems (mood swings, insomnia, etc.), Jones sought professional help that culminated in her undergoing hypnosis.

While under this hypnosis, Jones suddenly remembered having been a human guinea pig in CIA mind-control experiments throughout the 1960s. Subsequent investigation revealed that from 1960-1972 Jones had been the victim of CIA narcohypnosis (a combination of drugs and hypnosis), during which a CIA doctor effectively split her personality in two!

To accomplish this, the mad doctor used a variety of hypnosis induction methods including candles, a swinging pendulum, flashing lights, and monotonous "oriental" music. A variety of drugs were used to augment the process.

Candy Jones was not the only person to undergo such experimentation by the CIA. In *Trance Formation of America*, author Cathy O'Brien recounts her own experiences at the hands of CIA mind-slayers.[30] Successful mind-control experiments such as Jones' and O'Brien's encouraged covert government mind-manipulation Black-Ops such as the Government's MONARCH program, a.k.a. MK-ULTRA.

MK-ULTRA aimed to create subconsciously controlled couriers and assassins triggered by a secret code word (as in the Charles Bronson movie *Telefon*). Still another notorious government program involved attempts to create psychic killers!

Psychic Assassins

In 1995, the U.S. government acknowledged the existence of the secret program known by several names but finally as Stargate. This CIA-sponsored group of "psychic spies" operated from the mid-'60s up through 1988.

This secret unit of eight or more men was made up of recruits who had scored high on ESP tests. Taught to control their ESP ability through biofeedback, these psychics were initially employed to do "remote viewing" of "soft targets" (such as pinpointing the location of hostages and reading the minds of enemy leaders and scientists) and "hard targets" (such as locating hidden military installations).

Stargate was eventually discontinued, but not before attempts were made to turn Stargate's psychic spies into psychic assassins capable of using their ESP power to kill enemy leaders with a psychic bolt from afar![31]

During President George Bush's trip to Japan, it was alleged that Japanese intelligence used their own psychic assassins to make Bush sick enough to vomit during an important dinner, causing America to lose face in the eyes of the Japanese people. This would ensure Bush would then feel obligated to give economic and political concessions to Japan in order to recover his face. These Japanese psychic assassins reportedly employed an ancient ninja mind-control technique known as *ki-doll*.[32]

The Third Wave

> "You thought that you were the elect. That you were better than those outside this room. You bargained your freedom for the comfort of discipline and superiority. You chose to accept the group's will and the big lie over your own conviction. Oh, you think to yourself that you were just going along for the fun. That you could extricate yourself at any moment. But where were you heading? How far would you have gone?"
>
> —Ron Jones[33]

It took less than five days in April 1969 for teacher Ron Jones to turn 200 students at normal, middle-class Cubbely High School in Palo Alto, California into goose-stepping Nazis.

Jones' intent was to help students in his world history class understand the mentality of Nazi Germany. Jones planned to do this by having his class form "The Third Wave," a role-playing group complete with all the fascist trappings: easy-to-parrot slogans (Strength through Discipline, Strength through Action, Strength through Pride); pseudo-military rankings; even a Nazi-like salute.

Jones was shocked at how quickly students took to his new, strict, and arbitrary rules of conduct. He was also alarmed at how easily "normal," middle-class students accepted orders—without question—from an authority figure.

On the third day, Jones issued membership cards, three of which were marked with red "X"s to indicate that these three students had been singled out to be monitors responsible for ensuring that other Third Wave members followed the rules even while not in class.

While only three red-X monitors had been appointed, Jones soon discovered that half the class was spying on the other half!

Jones also opened Third Wave membership, encouraging his original class members to recruit other students from outside the class. By the end of the day more than 200 students at Cubberly had joined The Third Wave!

By now, students' Third Wave role-playing had begun to bleed over into their lives outside class. When some parents expressed concern, a local

Rabbi stepped up to give his blessing to Jones and The Third Wave. Soon, even the principal was observed giving the Third Wave salute.

Ironically, Third Wave students' academic skills improved noticeably during the experiment. Jones found the students more focused and eager to learn and do more. Belonging to the Third Wave gave the students identity and purpose. On the more ominous side, some students became totally lost in their Third Wave identities. One student went so far as assigning himself the job of "bodyguard" to Jones.

Jones himself began feeling increasingly uncomfortable with his role as leader of The Third Wave, finding himself slipping into the role of dictator. He decided to end the experiment after some Third Wave students began bullying those students who took The Third Wave too lightly.

Jones needn't have been surprised that middle-class students, even those raised in the "Land of the Free," should so easily embrace an authoritarian system.

The research of psychologist Erich Fromm (1900-1980) concluded that, given a choice between freedom and security, people will choose security every time. Fromm determined that the more freedom of choice a person has, the more anxiety that person has.

Fromm also found that most individuals take their identity from their association with others. Thus they tend to do what others around them are doing—they "go along to get along."

The Third Wave experiment also reinforced the findings of controversial '60s researcher Stanley Milgram (born 1933). Milgram's experiments, conducted at Yale in the early 1960s, concluded that, in obedience to authority, people would go to extremes, even to the extent of torturing others. When test subjects were ordered to administer electric shock to other students:

> "They trembled, sweated, and showed other signs of stress when "punishing" the student. Still, a large majority carried out Milgram's order, administering what they believed was great pain. This led Milgram to conclude that ordinary people will follow orders, if they come from a legitimate authority, in the same way as the Germans did when told by their Nazi leaders to commit atrocities against the Jews."[34]

Mind-slayers know full well how attractive promises of security, order, and power can be, whether offered to an individual, a disenfranchised minority, or an entire nation. It is therefore vital each of us do a realistic assessment of our own susceptibility to the seduction of the symbols, ploys, and promises of power routinely used by both mind-slayers in power, and by those mind-slayers striving to be in power.

Police Mind-Slayers
"By what methods do police obtain such an unbelievable percentage of confessions? Perhaps a goodly number of these confessions are false, elicited only by unfair, illegal, or reprehensible methods of interrogation."
—Philip G. Zimbardo[35]

Tyrannical police forces—domestic and military—have routinely used physical torture to obtain confessions from prisoners. Today, under more scrutiny from human rights groups, the badge-wearing mind-slayers serving such regimes have taken to using more subtle techniques of interrogation, such as drugs (truth serums, chemical pain enhancers), forced hypnosis, and brainwashing. One tried-and-true strategy still used by police worldwide is good old-fashioned psychological intimidation.

Police have always used psychology to break suspects. For ethical police, a keen insight into psychology helps them stay one step ahead of criminals, aids in hostage negotiations, and helps them convince criminals to confess.

Yet depending on who is wielding it—an ethical policeman or a ruthless mind-slayer—insight into the human psyche backed by the power of a badge can be either a valuable tool for getting at the truth or a fearsome weapon of humiliation, torture, and mind-manipulation.

Thus, it is important to study these techniques, if not to improve our own craft, then to protect ourselves from mind-slayers wielding these techniques.

Confession is Good for the Soul
In the United States today, 80 percent of all crimes are solved by confessions. While most American police have progressed from yesterday's crude "billy-club brainwashings" to more subtle psychological "beatings," contemporary mind-slayer interrogation techniques are no less effective and, in many instances, hardly less brutal than medieval thumbscrews.

Japan has an even higher confession rate than the United States: 90 percent. However, human rights groups allege that Japanese police extract confessions through interrogations that are often "brutal attempts to break suspects psychologically."[36]

Many psychologists maintain that all of us harbor deep-seated guilt feelings for real and imagined crimes and sins committed during childhood, making wringing a confession out of a suspect all the easier. This theory goes on to say that we all have something we want to confess, something we need to get off our chests. (Remember our enterprising Yakuza gangster in the section on the confidence man?)

Police interrogators know how important a feeling of guilt is when interrogating a suspect. Therefore, in lieu of outright arresting a suspect, the investigator invites the suspect to come along to the police station to help clear up a few things, or to help police find the "real" culprit in a mug-book.

By doing this, in effect police are asking the suspect to "volunteer" to go with the police.

Innocent individuals often comply because they don't want to look guilty, or simply as a knee-jerk reaction to having been conditioned all their lives to obey authority. This is also why innocent people foolishly waive their right to have an attorney present. (Police always imply that even thinking about getting a lawyer will make you appear guilty.)

"Volunteering" to go down to the station is the suspect's first act of giving in to the interrogator. When the subsequent "interview" turns against the suspect, the suspect is reminded how he "volunteered." This is the interrogator's way of making a suspect feel guilty and foolish for having placed himself in such a situation.

In places where physical torture is still the order of the day, women prisoners are forced to strip off their own clothing. This humiliation is designed to make the woman feel guilty of assisting in her own torture. Rapists also use this ploy—planting the seeds in their victim's mind that she didn't fight back hard enough, proving she "wanted it." These seeded doubts following so close on the heels of the rape trauma are why so many rapes go unreported.

Setting the Stage

In the same way the producers of a Broadway play begin with a plot, develop a script, then assemble the players and props, so to do police interrogators "set the stage" for their well-rehearsed play. But this play's purpose is to trap, trick, and—when necessary—terrorize suspects into making confessions.

All interrogators begin with preparatory techniques designed to soften up the suspect. First, police interrogators make sure they control the time and place of the interrogation. Ideally, a suspect is never interrogated in familiar surroundings. An isolated, windowless room is best, one that is quiet and free of distraction. The room should be empty except for a bare table and one or two hard chairs. Armless, straight-backed chairs permit the suspect's conscious and unconscious movements to be observed. The suspect is never allowed any "tension-relieving" activities (such as playing with pencils or paperclips, etc.) that would allow him to occupy his hands.

Suspects are forbidden to smoke. Cigarettes are allowed only when they can be used by interrogators as a bribe.

As much as possible, suspects are reduced to a child-like state. To accomplish this, suspects are forced to sit quietly and told not to speak unless spoken to. They must ask permission to go to the restroom. (To increase a suspect's discomfort, interrogators offer the suspect a soda pop or cup of coffee prior to a lengthy interrogation, knowing that sooner or later the suspect will have to beg permission to pee.)

Studying these techniques, it is not hard to imagine how they can be easily tailored to suit individual needs of mind-slayers to gain the upper hand over their victims.

During wartime, POWs are always stripped of their uniforms to symbolize their loss of identity and their separation from comrades and support network. Likewise, criminal suspects are never interrogated in the presence of anyone they know and can lean on for support. Any distinctive clothing (gang colors, etc.) are taken from them.

Police interrogators usually opt to wear civilian clothes rather than uniforms in order to look less threatening. Career criminals often feel a sense of false pride when interviewed by plainclothes detectives, as opposed to uniform officers. Such criminals are prone to brag.

Psychological Ploys
"Never again will you be capable of love, or friendship, or joy of living, or laughter, or curiosity, or courage, or integrity. You will be hollow. We shall squeeze you empty, and then we shall fill you with ourselves."
—George Orwell, *1984*

124

Once the stage is set, police interrogators begin reciting a well-rehearsed dialogue of psychological threats and promises designed to unnerve the suspect. A cutting at the edges ploy is used by reminding the suspect how ashamed he's made his mother, his friends and family; how he's "failed" his gang, his country, his "manhood."

Other tried-and-true police interrogation tactics include:

The Knowledge Bluff. Police pretend to possess more evidence of crimes than they actually have. To do this, interrogators reveal a few clues to the suspect (most often only guesses) and pretend to know more, inviting the suspect to "fill in the blanks."

Often police up the ante by staging a phony ID line-up, complete with false witnesses who "positively identify" the supect.

Bargaining Down. Involves police making a suspect believe he is being charged with crimes more serious than the one the interrogators are actually trying to get a confession for.

For example, a burglar might be told he is being charged with a murder committed at the same time the burglary (the actual crime being investigated) took place. The suspect's only alibi is to say he was committing a burglary at the time of the murder.

Lie-Detector Scams. One enterprising police interrogator bought a novelty rock designed to change color when warmed by the hand. Asking a suspect to hold the rock, the interrogator stuns the suspect by pointing out the fact that the "truth rock" is changing color because the suspect lied! Other interrogators have had naive suspects hold walkie-talkies or keep their hands on the metal chair they are sitting in, a chair the suspect is told is hooked up to a lie-detector.

Note: Many cults also use pseudo-lie-detector machines that supposedly reveal a recruit's "secret feelings" and "dark secrets." This implants doubts in the recruit's mind about his previous beliefs, his feelings toward friends and family, and can even make him question his sexuality. Having "discovered" these hidden problems, the cult then offers ways to help the recruit work through his problems.

Playing one suspect off another. This works when two or more suspects are involved in a crime. One suspect is told the other suspect is being released (implying his partner snitched on him).

Other ploys of this nature include the first suspect "accidentally" seeing an interrogator talking in hushed tones to the second suspect. Or, the second suspect hearing a stenographer being called to record his partner's "confession."

If all else fails, one suspect hears the sounds (either real or feigned) of a fellow suspect being beaten and is told he is next!

Limited Time Offers. These are given to suspects to pressure them into confessing.

Like cult recruiters and Madison Avenue pitch-masters, police interrogators know most people don't make good decisions under pressure, therefore suspects are pressured to take advantage of "a limited time offer," to strike a plea bargain—before the other suspect grabs the offer.

Good Cop/Bad Cop. This strategy works because the unfamiliar surroundings of a police station and interview room cause suspects to look around for a sympathetic face. Realizing this, police interrogators work in pairs, with one playing the role of "Bad Cop," acting rude and threatening, while his partner, "Good Cop," pretends to have sympathy for the suspect. If you've ever seen a movie or television show about cops, this ploy will be familiar to you.

Bad Cop is quick to pounce on any nervous tells: facial tics, fidgeting, sweating, bobbing Adam's apple, or veins popping out on the suspect's neck as "proof" the suspect is lying. The more Bad Cop points out these "signs of guilt" (real or made up), the more the signs actually appear!

When Bad Cop launches into an uncontrollable tirade or makes motions to physically abuse the suspect, Good Cop steps in and orders Bad Cop to back off. With Bad Cop out of the room, cooling off, Good Cop apologizes for Bad Cop's behavior and confides to the suspect how he wishes they would assign him someone else to work with before Bad Cop hurts another suspect and gets them both in trouble again.

Like the accomplished mind-slayers they are, both Good Cop and Bad Cop have learned to spot and exploit psychological fault lines.

Where Bad Cop uses fear to browbeat a suspect, Good Cop uses sympathy ploys. ("I'd have done the same thing in your situation.") Good Cop also appeals to the suspect's ego, "Only a smart guy could pull off a job like this."

Good Cop minimizes the seriousness of the crime and always leaves the suspect with ready-made excuses for his actions and creates opportunities for the suspect to "come clean." Good Cop uses a macho appeal, "It took some big cojones to pull off something like this!" and then watches the suspect for body language tells such as his unconsciously sitting up straighter when "complimented."

Conversely, Bad Cop mocks the suspect and questions the suspect's "manhood": "Why are you afraid to talk? Who are you scared of?" Where Good Cop is polite, Bad Cop takes every opportunity to derail the suspect's train of thought, interrupting in mid-excuse, making the suspect start over, always pointing out any inconsistencies in the suspect's alibi—frustrating the suspect at every turn.

Unscrupulous interrogators have always relied on torture—both physical and psychological. Ethical police interrogators on the other hand rely solely on psychological ploys. Individual mind-slayers are well acquainted with these police interrogation tactics and they often adopt and adapt these techniques to manipulate their victims.

Ironically, many of these criminal mind-slayers learned their mind-manipulation tactics by themselves spending time "in the box," i.e. by being subjected to intense police interrogation.

On a grander scale, the same psychological insights the ethical police at your local station house use to get at the truth can be used by ruthless police mind-slayers in a tyrannical regime to cower and control a whole nation.

Implanting False Memories

> "If we can't trust our own minds to tell us the truth,
> what is there left to trust?"
> —Loftus and Ketcham[37]

Recent scientific studies have proven what police interrogators and mind-slayers have always known: that it is possible to implant false memories into a person's head and thereby get even the most innocent person to confess to the most heinous of crimes.

The most infamous case in modern times involving police interrogation and memory manipulation took place in Olympia, Washington, in 1988. In a scenario straight out of Salem, Massachusetts 1692, two daughters (aged 18 and 22) accused their father of having molested them.

The two daughters "remembered" this history of abuse while attending a fundamentalist Bible camp, where a charismatic cult expert lectured on how prevalent Satanic ritual abuse was, even in good Christian families.

Encouraged by the fellow camp-goers stepping forward to "confess" they had been the victims of ritual Satanic abuse and feeling peer pressure to fit in, the oldest daughter stepped forward to proclaim that she, her sister, and her brothers had been molested by her father, in her case for more than 17 years!

Returning home to Olympia, the two girls told their stories to the local sheriff.

Their father, a church-going, upstanding member of the community, was invited down to the police station for questioning. After hours of continuous interrogation, the father confessed to being a "High Priest of Satan," to being a sodomizer of children and a willing participant in the murder, dismemberment, and cannibalization of infants. He even remembered being abused himself at age 4 or 5. The man's stories became increasingly bizarre: incorporating infant sacrifice, Satanic ritual, and bestiality.

Before long, the accused man's wife and his two sons were also "remembering" incidents of abuse. When their memories became sketchy, their preacher and the police investigators were there to encourage them.[38] When questioned about his abuse, one of the sons first denied it, then "remembered" it, and then recanted. Soon the second daughter upped the ante by implicating two of her father's poker buddies.

All these "memories" were later proven false.

Eventually the father would come to his senses and try to withdraw his confession, but his appeal fell on deaf judicial ears and he was sentenced to 20 years in prison.

Why would a man confess to such a heinous array of crimes he didn't commit, crimes that never happened?

Recall that false memories are more easily implanted when they are both traumatic and when they are planted by a trusted person. Both these prerequisites came into play during the father's interrogation.

First, the father trusted his police interrogators who, ironically, were his friends and colleagues (he was a chief civil deputy for the same sheriff's department investigating the allegations against him).

Second, the father trusted his daughters who he'd described to police as "good Christian girls" incapable of lying. (Therefore, they must be telling the truth about the molestations, the police countered!)

Third, police interrogators knew the father's beliefs and were able to use kyonin-no-jutsu to turn those beliefs against him.

Investigating detectives (trusted friends and authority figures to the man) played on the father's religious fervor, liberally loading their questions with religious references they knew the man would respond to.

The father's religious beliefs (i.e. superstitions) taught him that "demonic forces" were real and warned him that the Devil had not only the power to make people do something they wouldn't normally do, but also to make them forget they had done it. These fundamentalist beliefs were reinforced by a visiting minister (a trusted authority figure) who invited the man to "get it off his chest," reassuring the confused and traumatized Christian that "confession is good for the soul."

Ironically, the prosecution's case began falling apart when their own expert on cult mind control turned against them, convinced that the father was not guilty and that he had been led to confess through a combination of leading questions and suggestive comments.

Eventually all the allegations of "Satanic abuse" remained unproven and the charges were dropped against the man's two poker buddies. By then however, it was already too late since the father had pled guilty and received his sentence.

The real injustice of the Olympia case was that no one was ever called to account for implanting the false memories of abuse into the two daughter's minds in the first place.

How police ask questions can have as much impact as the actual questions they ask. Evidence shows that even the phrasing of questions can influence answers.[39] There is a big difference in a police investigator asking an accident witness "How fast was the blue car going when it slammed into the red car?" and his asking "Did you see the cars collide?" Such leading questions are called "priming," as in priming a water pump. Thus:

"No two interrogations are the same. Every interrogation is shaped definitively by the personality of the source—and of the interrogator, because interrogation is an intensely interpersonal process."
—*KUBARK Counterintelligence Interrogation* [40]

Interrogation Hypnosis
"Any spellbinder is part hypnotist."
—Hans Holzer[41]

It has often been pointed out how closely the typical police interrogation session resembles hypnosis. Police interrogators are trained to keep suspects isolated (minimizing distractions, forcing a suspect to focus on a single subject) and to use words and tone designed to lull the subject into a state of tranquility.[42]

In the Olympia, Washington, case, interrogators reportedly spoke in soft, soothing tones and constantly encouraged the suspect (their "friend") to relax. This strategy succeeded in lulling the man into a "trance-like state," where he began speaking in a "strange, faraway voice."

Torturous conditions such as dieté (extremes of diet), sleep deprivation, and stress—all of which are used routinely by police interrogators—have all been shown to induce hypnotic-like trance states in suspects.

According to KUBARK, the CIA's counterintelligence interrogation manual, the main purpose of interrogation hypnosis is not to get at the truth, but rather to help the subject "align himself with his interrogators." Once this is accomplished:

" . . . once the subject is tricked into believing that he is talking to a friend rather than foe, or that divulging the truth is the best way to serve his own purposes, his resistance will be replaced by cooperation. The value of hypnotic trance is not that it permits the interrogator to impose his will but rather that it can be used to convince the interrogatee that there is no valid reason not to be forthcoming."
—*KUBARK Counterintelligence Interrogation*[43]

Under hypnosis subjects become more compliant and hypersusceptible to leading questions, cues, and suggestions from police and other observers.[44]

An estimated 5 to 10 percent of the population is already highly suggestible, hence hypnotizable, and can shift instantly and almost imperceptibly from normal consciousness into a deep hypnotic trance state. Therefore a police interrogator (or a long-winded salesman, for that matter) might inadvertently trigger a hypnotic state in a person they are interviewing without being aware of it, causing that person to become more susceptible to their message. How much more so if the interrogator (or salesman) is a ruthless mind-slayer deliberately trying to lull his subject into a trance?

Attempts have even been made to use forced hypnosis to coerce confessions.[45] Such deliberate mind-manipulation is often a prelude to cult and government brainwashing.

Making a suspect think he has been hypnotized is the next best thing to actually hypnotizing him. For example, a suspect may be slipped a "silent drug" (i.e. a drug he is not aware he has been given) before being told he is about to be hypnotized. As the interrogator begins to speak and the drug begins to take effect, the suspect feels "warm," "sleepy," or feels a "tingling in his limbs" all indications (to him) that he is actually being hypnotized.

Such One-Eyed Snake hypnotism ploys often have the effect of relieving a suspect of responsibility, giving him a reason to confess. If a suspect consciously or subconsciously wants to talk, your "pretending" to hypnotize him can induce him to "pretend" to be hypnotized, giving him the excuse he needs to spill his guts and save his skin. (This follows Sun Tzu's advice of always leaving an enemy a face-saving way out.)

Hypnosis can also be used to make a person forget, to cloud and confuse his true memories.

Once a suspect is placed in a relaxed, receptive state, doubts can be planted in his mind. Post-hypnotic suggestions can also be given to deeply-entranced subjects to make them repress certain facts, or to forget altogether that they've been hypnotized.

Hypnosis designed to induce amnesia is often augmented with drugs. Drugs to accomplish this, such as lorazepam (which blocks all memory of surgical procedures) and others mixed in concoctions with LSD-25 were studied by the CIA.[46]

"Did I not tell you just now how we are different from the perse-
cutors of the past? We are not content with negative obedience,
not even with the most abject submission. When finally you surrender to us, it must be of your own free will."

—George Orwell, *1984*

"The Effectiveness of a threat depends not only on what sort of
person the interrogatee is and whether he believes that his ques-
tioner can and will carry the threat out but also on the interrogator's reasons for threatening."

—*KUBARK Counterintelligence Interrogation*

Often the mind-slayer's craft comes down to simply making threats.
Some of these threats are overt, some more subtle. For example, the Good
Cop's threats are always implied, the Bad Cop's threats overt.

Threats are effective with some personality types, useless with others.

INTERROGATION CHARACTER TYPES

Character type: The Orderly Type
Traits: Orderly and frugal; intellectual; reaches decisions slowly; uses "The Cause"
for self advancement; can rationalize turning traitor. Nurses grudges.
Stubborn. Hates authority.
Countertactics: Appear orderly when talking to him. Turn him against his superiors
(who have failed him).

Character type: The Optimistic Type
Traits: Happy-go-lucky; impulsive and inconsistent; drug user; hopeful. Avoids
responsibility and leaves self in the hands of "fate." Seeks reassurance.
Sometimes the youngest in the family.
Countertactics: Convince him that fate has turned against him. Make him place his hope in
you. Be his protector (Good Cop/parent).

Character type: The Greedy, Demanding Type
Traits: Attached to others, his loyalties will shift if he feels authority has let him
down. Thinks the world owes him something. Seeks substitute parents.
Countertactics: Threaten his support network. Be his father or big brother. Show concern.

Character type: The Self-Centered Type
Traits: Fearful, he compensates with false bravado. Lies. Brags and craves approval. Externally motivated. Vain, sensitive to criticism.
Countertactics: Pretend to be impressed by his daring. Play on his vanity. Accuse his superiors of abandoning him.

Character type: The Masochistic Type
Traits: Has a strong, cruel, unrealistic side. Needs to relieve guilt, to atone. Compulsive gambler who loses on purpose. May remain silent to invite punishment. Beware of false confessions.
Countertactics: Play on his guilt. Use "parental" scolding. Convince him that if he confesses, he will be punished and then reinstated.

Character type: The Fear-of-Success Type
Traits: Cannot tolerate success. Accident-prone, fantasy-prone, "Elephant-shit" artist. Blames others. May have a need to suffer. (See The Masochistic Type)
Countertactics: Feed his grandiose, "Elephant-shit" plans. Convince him others (superiors) are holding him back.

Character type: The Reality-Challenged Type (a.k.a. The Schizoid)
Traits: Lives in a fantasy world. Unrealistic image of self. Doesn't like "inferiors" questioning him. No lasting relationships. Often unaware of his own lying. "The Cause" is simply a means to an end.
Countertactics: Reinforce his fantasy world. Play on his need for approval. Then destroy his fantasy world.

Character type: The Unjustly Victimized Type (a.k.a. The Exception)
Traits: Feels he is the victim of a great injustice. Believes the world owes him. He will make demands for special treatment in exchange for turning traitor. His fight is against "The System," whose power he secretly envies. He is above the law.
Countertactics: Turn his hatred of "The System" around, showing him how he can finally be part of "The System" and share its power because he deserves special recognition. Turn him against his comrades who "abandoned" him.

Character type: The Normal Type
Traits: Exhibits various combinations of traits from the previous eight types.
Countertactics: Remain observant and flexible in your responses. Adjust approach as specific traits are identified.

The following are rules of thumb mind-slayers use when making threats:

- Implied threats are better than direct threats.
- Threats delivered coolly and quietly are most effective.
- Never threaten out of anger, especially in response to the subject's anger.
- Threats should include a "way out," a way for the victim to give you the information you want, or do the thing you are asking him to do, and still save themselves (their self-respect, their life, etc.).
- Threats attacking self-esteem are more effective than physical threats.
- The threat of death should be used sparingly. Care should be taken that the subject does not see death as a welcome release from suffering and/or shame, or that his death will make him a "martyr."
- The threat of futility convinces the subject that all his efforts to resist interrogation (and/or indoctrination) are ultimately useless, a waste of time and effort causing him (and others) needless hardship. For some people, the idea of throwing their lives away means nothing, so long as they are "remembered." For such people, to die in obscurity is worse than death.
- Cutting-at-the-edges threats use implied and explicit threats against a subject's support network (family, friends, etc.).

When making threats, the mind-slayer watches the victim closely for any response tells given away by the victim's face and/or body language. This allows the interrogator to gauge the effectiveness of overt threats, and to notice when the victim has realized the implications of more covert threats.

How Propaganda Became a Dirty Word

"The function of propaganda does not lie in the scientific training of the individual, but in the calling of the masses' attention to certain facts, processes, necessities, etc., whose significance is thus for the first time placed in their field of vision."

—Adolf Hitler, *Mein Kampf*

Since World War II, propaganda has been a dirty word. Yet the concept of propaganda is hardly a 20th century invention:

"No doubt propaganda has existed ever since primates have been sufficiently articulate to use it. Artifacts from prehistory and from early civilizations give evidence that dazzling raiment, mystic insignia, and monuments were used to advertise the purported majesty and supernatural powers of early rulers and priests."[47]

Thus, propaganda as a tool and weapon of both religious and government policy has been known and used since ancient times.

If you happen to be a conqueror preferring to win territory by scaring people rather than having to skewer them, then the propaganda you send ahead of your army makes such conquest all the easier.

Persian dictator Cyrus the Great used propaganda against Babylon and Xerxes used it against the Greeks. Alexander the Great's father Philip II of Macedon also used it against Athens. Likewise, Genghis Khan's conquests were to a great extent aided by the propaganda (fear!) that rode ahead of his horde, warning of the futility and fatality of resisting the coming wave.

Ancient propaganda ploys concentrated on spreading myths and legends of a king's invincibility. Little has changed.

The most successful political and religious leaders either had a natural talent for propaganda or were smart enough to employ wily advisors adept at crafting and spreading easily memorized political slogans, or religious parables, proverbs, and commandments from their particular gods—all meant to excite and/or cower the people.

Propaganda and the Art of War
> "How to influence people was an old quest long
> before Dale Carnegie wrote about it."
> —Hans Holzer[48]

Our modern word "propaganda" comes from the Congregatio de Propaganda Fide (Congregation for the Propagation of the Faith), "The Propaganda" for short, a powerful group of cardinals in charge of promoting the Roman Catholic Church since 1622.

As the "art" of war became more sophisticated, systematic approaches to propaganda began appearing.

In China Sun Tzu understood the importance of propaganda when he wrote, "All warfare is based on deception."

In 4th century BCE, roughly around the same time Sun Tzu was penning his *Art of War*, a man named Kautilya, who was a Brahmin prime minister to the Nanda kings of Magadha, India, felt unappreciated by his employers and frustrated by their shortsightedness. He packed his bags and defected to their rival, Candragupta Maurya.

Candragupta was wiser than the Nanda, and recognized the wisdom of Kautilya's advice. Using Katilya's insights, Candragupta quickly swallowed up the lands of the Nanda and become emperor.

Kautilya eventually wrote his thoughts down into the *Arthasatra* (*Principles of Politics*), a treatise on the art of governing that is often compared with Plato's *Republic* and Machiavelli's *The Prince*. The *Arthasastra* discourses on both politics and economics.

Kautilya asserted that moral considerations have no place in politics and championed the use of spies, psychological warfare, and propaganda. According to Kautilya, propaganda, both overt and covert, should be used to disrupt an enemy's army and capture his capital:

> "He advised the king to follow only that policy calculated to increase his power and material resources, and he felt no scruple in recommending dubious and sometimes highly unjust and immoral means to achieve that end. For this purpose he sketched an elaborate system for recruiting spies and training them."[49]

Covertly, propaganda agents should be sent to infiltrate the kingdoms of both present and potential enemies: spreading defeatist gloom and doom among enemy troops; planting rumor and misleading news (a.k.a. "disinformation") among enemy civilians:

"Like modern propagandists, Kautilya was much preoccupied with techniques for sowing fear, dissension, and confusion in the opponent's ranks (psychological warfare) and for showering blandishments on allies without becoming excessively dependent upon them."[50]

Overtly, propagandists raise the standard of the king as high as possible: proclaiming the king to be the embodiment of all that is good, convincing the people that the king can do magic, announcing that God and the Prophets are all on the king's side! Within the king's own kingdom, internal propaganda is used to manipulate a king's subjects in order to stimulate their support for state policies.

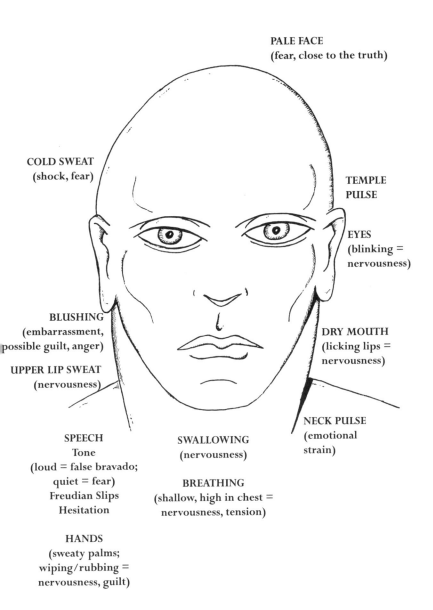

PALE FACE
(fear, close to the truth)

COLD SWEAT
(shock, fear)

TEMPLE
PULSE

EYES
(blinking =
nervousness)

BLUSHING
(embarrassment,
possible guilt, anger)

DRY MOUTH
(licking lips =
nervousness)

UPPER LIP SWEAT
(nervousness)

SPEECH
Tone
(loud = false bravado;
quiet = fear)
Freudian Slips
Hesitation

SWALLOWING
(nervousness)

NECK PULSE
(emotional
strain)

BREATHING
(shallow, high in chest =
nervousness, tension)

HANDS
(sweaty palms;
wiping/rubbing =
nervousness, guilt)

According to Kautilya, a king has two goals: to keep himself in power, and to ensure the prosperity of the people (thereby safeguarding his own position). All propaganda is therefore intended to teach a simple lesson: All who support the king's goals will reap great benefit. All who oppose the king will reap the whirlwind!

This is why Kautilya is often referred to as "the Eastern Machiavelli."

Systematic approaches to propaganda appeared in the West as early as Athens, 500 BCE. But not until the notorious Florentine Niccolo Machiavelli (1469-1527) penned *The Prince* (1513) and *The Art of War* (1520), outlining how to ruthlessly gain and then maintain power, was propaganda seen as a vital and indispensable part of both military and political conflict.

Considered by many to be "the father of modern political science," Machiavelli wrote that a ruler was justified in using any means necessary to maintain the stability of his lands, including cruelty, force, and deception (i.e. propaganda).

According to Machiavelli, a virtuous prince maintains power not by crushing his subjects when they rise against him, but by preventing his subjects from becoming rebellious. To accomplish this, the prince utilizes propaganda and the institutions of religion to keep the people satisfied.

Machiavelli became required reading and his writings influenced not only ambitious political and religious leaders, but social philosophers and even playwrights.

While works of fiction, many of the plays of William Shakespeare (1564-1616) reveal an astute familiarity with the use of psychological warfare and propaganda.

In *King Richard III* (1591), Buckingham plants rebel-rousers in town to stir popular support for Richard's coup. In another propaganda ploy, Richard leaves a note on Norfolk's tent prior to battle meant to undermine Norfolk's morale. And prior to the Battle of Bosworth Field, Richard gives a propaganda-laden speech, inciting his men, assuaging their consciences and destroying their doubts.

Similarly stirring was *King Henry V*'s (1600) inspiring speech to the king's men prior to Agincourt, goading them to victory. In *Hamlet* (1603), the depressed Prince of Denmark puts on a play to unnerve his traitorous uncle. What are Iago's whispered rumors and the suggestions of infidelity he successfully planted in the mind of the Moor in *Othello* (1622) if not propaganda?

Mark Anthony's rebel-rousing, sarcastic speech in *Julius Caesar* (1623) gradually turns the crowd of listeners into a mob ready to burn and kill in order to avenge Caesar's assassination. *Macbeth* (1623) sees a man led astray by the prophecy-propaganda of three witches and by the whispers of his ambitious wife.

Today, propaganda is an intrinsic factor in any military campaign. Yet we need not be attached to the military to be affected by it. Each of us are also affected on a daily basis by propaganda beamed at us by a variety of groups, some political, some religious, many with questionable, shadowy, and downright dangerous agendas.

Whatever their goals—obvious or hidden, global or backyard—the same tried-and-true tactics and techniques of propaganda are used by all such mind-slayers.

Types of Propaganda

"The proper words can make people take actions. 'Sticks and stones can break my bones, but words . . . ?' Wrong. Words can do all sorts of things. For instance, words of praise can make you work harder, run faster, or behave in a jollier way. A word of criticism can do the opposite. Whether or not we believe the words, they do their work. 'Something always sticks' is the way the Romans put it. The word, being an externalization of a thought, is the key to our behavior."
—Hans Holzer

Propaganda attacks all three of Sigmund Freud's classic levels of mind:

- Rational and logical arguments engage the Ego;
- Pleasurable promises appeal to our child-like Id; and
- Moral arguments target the higher reasoning Super-Ego.

Propaganda arguments fall into two categories, depending on their intended target audience. Strategic propaganda is aimed at a mass audience, and carries a more generalized message (e.g. the enemy is a bad person). Tactical propaganda, on the other hand, is more specific, more finely tuned and aims to get us do specific things (e.g. buy this car, buy this war).

Where strategic propaganda uses commonly shared symbols and universal archetypes that affect everyone (e.g. all Americans), tactical propaganda uses the same images in addition to images and symbols that have special meaning within a specifically-targeted group (e.g. a minority or a specific religious group).

Whether strategic or tactical, all propaganda must be adjusted to the particular level of understanding of those being targeted:

"All propaganda must be popular and its intellectual level must be adjusted to the most limited intelligence among those it is addressed to." (Adolf Hitler, *Mein Kampf*)

Thus, depending on its intent and intended audience, a typical propaganda ploy can include the use of suggestions (overt and subliminal), innuendo, and rumor on both a personal and/or mass scale. In other words, propaganda is just a rumor on steroids.

In *The Encyclopedia of Human Behavior*, author R.M. Goldenson, Ph.D., defines a rumor thus:

"An unverified report or account that circulates primarily by word of mouth. Rumors may be wholly false or may contain an element of truth that is usually distorted or exaggerated. Though they often circulate in the form of gossip and may be deliberately 'planted' at any time, they tend to occur in greatest profusion during periods of public crisis when reliable information is hard to obtain."[51]

Whether spread thin by individual mind-slayers or slathered on thick by professional government spin-doctors, rumors are the butter on the bread of propaganda.

All concerted programs of propaganda begin as rumors. Some are deliberately planted by mind-slayers in preparation for future propaganda, while others occur spontaneously (in lieu of real information being available) and are helped along by mind-slayers.

The classic office rumor goes something like this: You casually mentions to the office gossip that "Bob certainly seems to be doing better since he finished the program . . ." Then you quickly change the subject when asked "What program?"

Drug problems? Emotional problems? Marital problems? No one seems to be sure, and you can bet they aren't going to ask "Poor Bob." Just to be on the safe side, not wanting to upset Bob, they start avoiding the troubled man.

The boss, having heard the rumor, may decide to take it easy on Bob 'till

Bob works out his problems. The boss then assigns Bob's pet project to the next man in line . . . you!

The more sketchy a rumor the better. Rumors work best when you allow others to fill in the blanks.

Tools of Propaganda

Propaganda aims to accomplish one of two goals: Integration propaganda helps form people into more easily manageable units, causing them to hold the same opinion about a specific thing. This makes it easier to control them and, when need be, to focus their collective energies against the enemy. Agitation propaganda incites us to do a specific action.

Both integration propaganda and agitation propaganda use one or more of the following arguments:

- Us versus them: There is no middle ground. They are different than us. They don't think like us, ergo They are less deserving of life and land than us.
- Taboo and terror: They have committed atrocities—crimes against humanity. They trample our traditions and commit taboo acts shocking to both man and God.
- Exaggeration: The number of the dead killed and oppressed by our enemy are purposely inflated to make matters sound worse than they really are. Statistics are skewed. Someone once said that if you torture numbers long enough, they'll confess to anything!
- High stakes: We are shown how we will be directly affected by any failure on our part to act. Our children are at risk! Our way of life is being threatened!
- Demonization: The enemy isn't human. He is a Godless beast, or he is subhuman. His barbaric acts have cost him his humanity (thus he can be slain and his lands seized without any guilt attaching itself to us).
- God is on our side: We are good, they are evil. God loves us more than he loves them.
- Turnabout's fair play: They did it to us, we are justified in doing it to them. This is also where you turn an enemy's propaganda against him, using his own words to indict him.

What makes these propaganda arguments so effective is that they all contain a little bit of the truth. Humans have a lazy habit of thinking that if A, B, and C are true, D must also be true. Mind-slayers count on this. Hide little lies inside a big truth. Wrap big lies in a lot of little truths.

Techniques of Propaganda
> "To influence the masses rather than one single subject is of course more difficult, but certain key words, slogans, tones of voice, and emotional circumstances are all part of the hypnotists' "one-step . . . two-step . . . three-step" formula; it is just applied to a broader audience."
> —Hans Holzer[52]

For propaganda to be successful, mind-slayers must determine their audience's mind-set, including their susceptibility to physical and psychological inducements (i.e. threats and bribery).

First, what is likely to be your audience's initial attitude to your strategic, overall message? Does the targeted audience have a predisposition to the message you are offering? Is it something they (secretly) want to hear? Your message is designed to replace the person's present belief. Does it strike a chord with him? Have you been sure to wrap any bitter message pills in sweet propaganda—easy-to-swallow symbols and phrases the audience recognizes, identifies with, and has been known to respond favorably to in the past?

Second, what inducements (bribes or threats) does your offer carry? In other words, what does the audience have to gain or lose psychologically and/or physically by accepting your message?

This includes economic inducements, bribes of money, and lucrative job opportunities on the one hand, threats of losing the same on the other hand. Physical inducements can also include promises of security, sex, and material wealth.

Psychological inducements people are most likely to respond to include offers for fulfillment of personal (perhaps secret) desires, promises of recognition, promises of increased social acceptance, prestige and power. At the opposite extreme, your propaganda can threaten to take all these things away if your agenda is not embraced.

Common propaganda ploys to accomplish this include:

- Identification ploys. The mind-slayer goes out of his way to identify himself and his cause with the common man, plain folks—anything to win the hearts and minds of his audience.
- Argumentum ad Populum (argument to the people). Mind-slayers frame their appeals in everyday language meant to appeal to the common folk and common sense.
- Bandwagon ploys. These assure us "Everyone is doing it" and we don't want to be left out, do we? This appeals to our need to be accepted, to be part of the crowd.
- Testimonial ploys. Present us with famous people (war heroes, movie stars, sports figures) who entice us to buy what they're endorsing.
- Transfer ploys (a.k.a. guilt by association). A cutting-at-the-edges ploy in which you are attacked for the company you keep and held suspect by your associations.
- Name-calling ploys. These label others as bleeding hearts, communists, Godless pagans, or use other societal taboo slur words.
- Stroking ploys. The opposite of name-calling ploys, these use societal prestige words, terms such as patriot, true American, and "an example to us all" to attract and flatter members of the target audience.
- Purr Generality ploys. Rather than stick to the facts and address specific solutions to specific problems, generality ploys use emotional pleas and speak in vague terms. They use evocative but unclear terms like justice, family values, motherhood, and other societal virtue words to jerk our chains.
- Slur Generality ploys. Slur generalities include New-Ager, pagan, godless, and occult catchalls. (We're not sure exactly what these terms mean, but we know they can't be good!) Politicians are often accused of being soft on crime, although there is no specific definition for the general slur "soft."
- Faulty reasoning ploys. Include use of faulty cause and effect, false analogy, and defective comparison. The statement "Crime has risen 90 percent since he took office" may be true, but no connection—cause and effect—has actually been established.
- Assumption ploys (a.k.a. "begging the question"). The mind-slayer puts

out the notion that "No one in his right mind would support such an unfeasible plan." Has it been *shown* to be "unfeasible" or are we being asked to *assume* it is unfeasible?

- Selective memory (a.k.a. lying by omission). We're all pretty good at remembering what bolsters our own agendas, forgetting to mention pertinent facts that reveal the downsides of our agendas. Mind-slayers using reasoning ploys are notorious for having selective memories .
- Pressure ploys. These force listeners to choose between two extremes (e.g. between good and evil), with no compromise allowed to be considered. A cult's "limited time offer" falls into this category.
- Semantics ploys. Use plays on words (homonyms, vague definitions, etc.) to confuse and wear down their audience.
- Argumentum ad Hominem ("argument to the man"). When all else fails, propaganda attacks are made against the person himself, whether he is a candidate running for office or the salesman endorsing a rival product.

Ninja Use of Propaganda

The shinobi-ninja understood the need for, and the effectiveness of, propaganda in both peacetime and war.

Shinobi propaganda included perpetuating the belief—both to recruits and to outsiders—that ninja were descended from demons; that they were unbeatable warriors who could walk through walls; that they possessed the secret of the death touch.

The effectiveness of these kyonin-no-jutsu propaganda ploys is evident in the fact that, still today, when the word "ninja" is spoken, people both East and West conjure up an image in their mind of mysterious shadow-warriors capable of killing with a single touch!

Spreading tales added to the fear in which their foes held them, increasing safety for the whole clan. The individual exploits—the "personal propaganda"—of any single ninja increased the awe in which the whole clan was held.

Personal Propaganda

"An agitator who demonstrates the ability to transmit an idea to
the broad masses must always be a psychologist,
even if he is only a demagogue."
—Adolf Hitler, *Mein Kampf*

What is the future of propaganda?

According to some experts, tomorrow's mind-slayer media manipulators will move away from propaganda aimed at mass audiences and more toward crafting different versions of a message for each audience segment (race, demographic). This is known as "The Dear Mary" approach and is already used by direct marketing copywriters. As technology increases and privacy decreases, mind-slayers armed with data from credit card and tax records, medical data bases, and other sources will be able to target individuals with propaganda personalized to suit that particular individual.

Wherever the person turns, he will be confronted in print (such as newspapers or magazines he subscribes to), via television shows he watches regularly, through the video games he plays, and at the Web sites he most frequents.

For example: You set your clock-radio to awaken you at 7:30 a.m. and the moment it comes on you hear a message targeting you specifically with a subtle—perhaps subliminal—message in the form of an ad or a piece of news. At the newsstand, your favorite newspaper and/or magazines carry a cover story of the same news or a blatant ad for the same product. The placard on the side of the bus you take every day to work or on that billboard alongside the same road you drive to work holds the same message.

These media masters are already "laying in wait" to ambush you at work, having already used a cutting-at-the-edges approach to make sure all your co-workers are standing around the water-cooler talking about the same news or product.[53]

Even today, think how easy it is for a propaganda message to be infiltrated into entertainment. For example, how many times a day do you hear-repeated the joke Jay Leno told last night?

If this is indeed the future of propaganda, then what does the future hold for individuals in regard to propaganda? Scant, unless we learn to master propaganda before its masters master us!

We start by reminding ourselves that our reputations precede us. How many times have we been warned to watch out for a particular salesman, an opposing attorney, or even a rival ball team, simply because they are known to be tough customers? *That* is propaganda!

Remember, ancient Celtic shaman cultivated a power called "glamour," an overpowering personal presence that, coupled with specially chosen words, could accomplish dazzling effects, from disrobing a lover to disarming an enemy. Our "personal propaganda" works in this same way. At the most basic level, our personal propaganda is how we carry ourselves: our walk of alertness that turns aside muggers, our air of confidence that makes the salesman lower his price.

How we carry ourselves tells the world we are tough customers—that we won't put up with their bullshit. Word gets around and the wolves no longer come sniffing at our door.

For the most part, criminal mind-slayers are a mangy lot, culling the human herd by targeting the weak and the unwary. By studying the tactics of these human hyenas, we make ourselves less of a target for their mind-manipulation ploys. (Recommended reading: *Winning Through Intimidation* by Robert J. Ringer.[54])

Coming Clean about Brainwashing
"Although brainwashing is a comparatively recent addition to the armory of political weapons, it has many points of similarity, both in behavioral manifestations and in psychological dynamics, to phenomena with which the Western world is quite familiar. Among these are spontaneous religious conversions, voodoo rites, hypnosis, conditioned reflex behavior, and of course, the extraction of confessions from 'witches' in earlier centuries."[55]

All of us maintain those beliefs and behaviors that are most helpful to us in any given environment. These beliefs and behaviors are first and foremost functional; they help us survive and get along with others.

When conditions change—or we are tricked into believing conditions have changed—we survive by changing our behavior.

Our beliefs determine our behaviors. Our behaviors, in turn, reflect our beliefs. What we do, we become.

Change a man's beliefs and you change his behavior.

Convince him to do things he wouldn't normally do and you begin to change his beliefs, both about himself and the world.

Brainwashing therefore aims at first convincing us our present beliefs and behaviors are not functional, thus convincing us to throw away those beliefs and behaviors and adopt the "suggestions" being fed to us on what we should believe and how we should behave.

In modern times, horror stories of Communist Chinese trying to sub-vert and indoctrinate NATO POWs during the Korean War brought the word "brainwashing" to worldwide attention.

Reportedly, Communist Chinese had been using various brainwashing techniques against enemy soldiers and civilians as early as the 1920s. Such techniques have long been known in China and some can be traced as far back as the moshuh nanren.

The Soviets also experimented with such techniques, giving Western countries the justification they needed to carry out their own brainwashing experiments. It is now common knowledge that U.S. intelligence agencies like the CIA poured millions into brainwashing research.

In his book *Crusade: Undercover against the Mafia and KGB*, author Tom Tripodi, a 27-year veteran CIA agent and undercover narcotics officer, admits to a consensus among CIA agents that "The Company" had at its dis-posal the resources for what is commonly called brainwashing.[56]

Since 1954, brainwashing techniques have greatly improved, becoming more refined due in part to the rise in modern mind-altering drugs and elec-tronic mind-control machines.

What is Brainwashing?

Brainwashing has been defined as: intensive propaganda techniques that are applied under conditions of stress and/or coercive persuasion, during which an individual is confronted by conditions deliberately designed to undermine his morale and make him question his accepted attitudes. This paves the way for indoctrination with a "replacement set of beliefs" that will produce a change in behavior.[57]

Using this definition, we find that political education, religious indoc-trination, and general socialization can all be said to contain elements of brainwashing since all three have the same basic goal: to replace a person's present beliefs and behaviors with beliefs and behaviors more in line with the agenda of whomever is doing the brainwashing.

To accomplish this, mind-slayers use reason and logic, evoke emotion, make appeals to faith, use psychological persuasion and, when need be, use physical coercion to change a person's behavior.

They do this by first breaking the person down and then rebuilding him in the brainwasher's image.

Phase One: Breakdown

Breakdown undermines the person's morale, causing the person targeted to begin to doubt, making him question his accepted beliefs and behaviors. This phase of the brainwashing process uses both physical and psychological tactics.

Physical breakdown is accomplished by assuming as much control over the body of the person targeted as possible. In extreme cases, such as with POWs or cult recruits, a person's movement is physically restricted and all their "intimate needs" (eating, bathing, using the toilet) are controlled by the brainwasher in order to bring about a feeling of powerlessness in the person.

Isolation is used two ways during this initial phase. First, the subject is kept cut off from outside information and influence. Second, actual physical isolation and/or enforced silence (solitary confinement) makes the brainwashee more eager to join a re-eduction group or thought reform class, if only to experience some human contact.

Psychological breakdown then takes a person already weakened in body by physical mistreatment—exhaustion, meager diet, sleep deprivation, and torture—and attacks his mind.

Psychological attack often begins with humiliation: first stripping the person of his dignity, and then offering to restore that lost dignity bit-by-bit in exchange for cooperation. Forced to remain naked and filthy for days, a POW is grateful to the "kind" interrogator offering him a shower and giving him clothes to wear, helping him restore a little of his lost dignity.

This is the brainwasher's foot-in-the-door: first he creates doubt in the subject's previously held truths, then he offers the brainwashed subject "new truths."

Planting doubt in the subject's mind begins with seeding small uncertainties about such things as the day and time or even who is winning the war.

Little uncertainties lead to big doubts, to distrust of past beliefs, opening the subject up to future changes in attitudes.

The mind-slayer does this by showing the subject with new variables, previously unseen connections, and heretofore unimagined considerations (e.g. how their former political and religious leaders lied to them, how they were involved in an unjust war, how to see reality from their new-found "friend's" point of view). Eventually doubt takes root: doubts of self-worth, doubts in comrades and country. Doubt becomes resentment, then becomes anger that his government and God are unable to protect or rescue him from harm. Weakened in body and mind, under constant bombardment of the interrogator's "facts," the brainwashee's former self-image (of being invincible and of being valued by his country) begins to crumble.

The interrogator's job is to recognize and then voice what the captive is thinking by this time: that they have been forgotten, even betrayed by country and comrades. Such doubts often cause captives to actually identify with their captors. (This attitude is known as "The Stockholm Syndrome.")

Previously brainwashed prisoners can be used to help break down their fellow prisoners. Such peer pressure is highly effective, especially when coming from a respected figure (friends, commanding officer).

Phase Two: Build-Up

Build-up then introduces the subject to a new set of beliefs and behaviors. Techniques of brainwashing indoctrination include both physical controls and psychological attacks such as those already discussed in the section on The Cult Craft.

Their old identity shattered, the sympathetic brainwasher offers the broken brainwashee a new, more functional identity.

In a cult or POW indoctrination situation, the brainwasher sometimes asks the person to just "pretend" to cooperate (so that the brainwasher won't be accused of failing and get into trouble with his superiors). In return for the brainwashee's role-playing, the brainwasher promises him special rewards, perhaps even the promise of escape in the future.

To quote the Brainwasher's Bible chapter and verse:

Saying is believing.

Believing leads to behaving.

What we do, we become.

It is a short step from "pretending" to be a traitor or a cult member to forgetting you're only role-playing.

We must learn to recognize the signs of brainwashing—whether by cults, police or by other government entities—both in order to guard our loved ones and ourselves.

Psychotronics

"One must concede at least the possibility that technological advances may someday . . . remold the human mind on the same mass scale and with the same economy and efficiency which advances in nuclear technology have enabled us to use in dealing with the human body."[58]

—International Encyclopedia of Social Sciences

The inherently dangerous nature of their lives demanded that medieval shinobi-ninja keep up on the latest innovations—whether the latest tactic for penetrating an enemy stronghold, or the latest technique for penetrating a foe's mind castle.

As vital as it was in medieval times for mind-slayers to keep up on the latest technological developments, it's all the more important to do so in a time when technology is changing on a daily basis. Thus, for the survival of their dark craft, modern mind-slayers keep abreast of the latest psychotronic advances for peering into the mind and/or for augmenting their already fearsome mind invasion prowess.

Psychotronics is the applied science of influencing, controlling and/or destroying the human mind via electronic devices.

On the one hand, the electronic augmentation of the human mind holds the promise of helping us expand our own minds (our awareness, memory, etc.). However, in the hands of ruthless mind-slayers, misuse of psychotronics holds sinister possibilities for mind-manipulation and mental enslavement.

This is not the stuff of future fiction. Serious attempts have already been made by individuals, by cults, and by governments (our own included) to use psychotronics to influence and control the minds of both individuals and the masses.

Lie-detection

Despite the fact that polygraph experts disagree as to the accuracy of modern polygraph machines, and despite the fact that polygraph results are not admissible in courts of law, each year hundreds of thousands of Americans are nonetheless subjected to polygraph interrogations, not only during criminal investigations but, increasingly, as part of pre-job screenings.[59] Today the polygraph remains the most widely used method for psychotronic lie-detection.

Some have beaten the polygraph through the use of another "psychotronic" device, the biofeedback machine, which teaches them to control heartbeat, respiration, pulse, and skin conductivity—the indicators the polygraph relies on.

Less known and not as widely used as the polygraph is the CVSA— "Computer Voice-Stress Analyzer." The CVSA has been called "high-tech truth serum" and has been praised as the replacement for the polygraph. While only recently in the news, the CVSA was proposed as a lie-detection tool more than 25 years ago.

During the 1960s, the U.S. Defense Department spent countless dollars developing electronic devices for secretly detecting when someone was lying. These devices measured body stress without a person's knowledge. One such device, the "wiggle seat," measured tiny movements made by a sitting subject. Another device used an infrared detector to measure the heat of a person's upper lip.

Note that all the tells measured by devices such as the polygraph and the wiggle seat can be spotted by alert mind-slayers using only their five senses. We can see fidgeting, a flushed face and a sweating upper lip on someone we are talking to. We can also see, and in some cases hear, changes in a person's breathing. We can even note changes in a person's pulse and heart rate by shaking his hand and touching the inside of his wrist, and check his heart rate by either observing arteries on the side of his neck or by placing our hands on his back or on his shoulder (touching the sub-clavicle artery under the collar-bone).

Hypnopaedia

The theory of sleep learning has been around for decades. In Aldous Huxley's dark vision of the future, *Brave New World* (1932), sleep learning— actually sleep indoctrination and brainwashing—is called "hypnopaedia" and operates on the same theory as subliminal suggestion.

Studies testifying to the truth of sleep learning show that it works best when we are trying to modify lower-level behaviors and improve physical skills as opposed to trying to acquire higher-level skills such as learning a language.

We already know the human voice alone can be used to heal, hurt, and hypnotize. For example, it has been estimated that the frequency of Adolf Hitler's voice in a typical sentence from one of his speeches was 228 vibrations per second, whereas 200 vibrations is the usual frequency of a voice raised in anger.[60]

A typical Hitler speech started quietly, gradually rising to a crescendo and then stopping abruptly, with the "punch line" delivered in a loud, sometimes hoarse and high-pitched voice.

To exploit Hitler's "gift," the Nazis ordered German radio manufacturers to place a radio in every German home. As a result, by 1939, 70 percent of all German households owned a wireless set, the highest percentage anywhere in the world, including the United States. Listening to Nazi radio propaganda was mandatory. In addition to radios in the home, loudspeakers were placed in all factories, and work stopped whenever Hitler spoke. Nazi plans to install 6,000 loudspeaker pillars in streets nationwide—first pioneered by the Soviets, by the way—was interrupted by the War.[61]

While Nazi attempts at using psychotronics (i.e. radio waves) to disseminate propaganda were effective for their time, they were naive by today's standards. (Imagine what Hitler could have accomplished with MTV!)

This kind of saturation propaganda employs the same principle as hypnopaedia. In the case of pervasive Nazi propaganda, since there was no escaping it, people began ignoring it on a conscious level. However, the insidious messages continued to burrow into their subconscious minds, subtly influencing them over time.

In the same way, sleep-learning enters our subconscious brains while our "higher" conscious brain is "asleep." This explains why sleep-learning is more effective for teaching physical skills (controlled by the lower brain).

The Russian Device

In 1993 a top FBI scientist admitted proposing the use of an experimental Russian "mind control device" against David Koresh during the standoff in Waco.[62]

Reportedly, just a few weeks before 80 Branch Davidians died in the Waco fire, a small group of American Military Intelligence and law-enforcement officials in Washington witnessed a demonstration of a device that was designed to control people by implanting thoughts in their minds. According to its Russian creator, the device could subconsciously alter Koresh's behavior by sending the cult leader a subliminal message over the telephone while the FBI was negotiating with him.[63]

The Russian Device first used an electroencephalograph (EEG) to measure brain waves during various emotional moods (such as anger or excitement). Subliminal messages could then be recorded at the same frequency as a previously mapped out "mood." Hearing these "matched" subliminal messages would then produce the same mood in the listener.

If this sounds familiar, that's because it's the same process mind-slayers use —minus the electronic device—when mirroring their victims' speech and body language.

In a bizarre variation of this, members of Japan's Aum Shinri Kyo death cult reportedly paid $115,000 a piece for headsets that were supposed to let them tune into their leader Asahara's brainwaves, thus "matching" their brainwaves to his.

In the wrong hands, the inventor of The Russian Device admits his device—and, conceivably, other such devices—could be used to push people into violent acts. Still, he waxes philosophic: "A knife can be used to cut sausage, or cut your throat."[64]

The U.S. government eventually decided not to use The Russian Device. Still, the potential for the use or misuse of such technology is obvious. As one writer put it: "If David Koresh now, who next?"[65]

The Electro-Magnetic Enemy

Russian research into psychotronic devices is nothing new, nor was their 1993 offer the first time Russian scientists tried to peddle such a device in America. In the early 1980s, Soviet scientists offered the United States "The Lida," a mind-control device that broadcast radio waves attuned to the frequency of deep-sleep EEGs. The Russian scientists claimed they had used The Lida successfully on human beings to treat insomnia, anxiety, hypertension, and other neurosis. When demonstrated on an agitated cat, The Lida zapped the cat into a docile trance.

There were rumors at the time of a more sophisticated version of The Lida capable of controlling minds at a distance.[66]

The Lida was engineered around the fact that a person's brain waves tend to "mimic" surrounding electromagnetic frequencies. Thus, applying different hertz (hz) frequencies can produce different mental states ranging from drowsiness to transcendental serenity."[67]

For example, Extremely Low Frequency (ELF) waves up to 100 hz are not normally noticed by our unaided senses, yet they have been shown to cause both physical and emotional disorders.

Infrasound vibrations (up to 20 hz) can subliminally cause our brains to align with Alpha, Beta, Theta, or Delta (sleep) wave patterns, producing moods in a listener ranging from alertness to passivity.

Infrasound generators using very low frequency sound waves have already been tested by France and other nations for crowd control. A beam from one of these generators makes people fall to the ground vomiting and shitting on themselves.[68]

ELF sound waves that provoke nausea and vomiting and disrupt orientation have effectiveness estimated at 1,600 miles.

California neurologists have found a way to focus ultrasonic waves into a beam of vibrations capable of affecting the brain's neurons, thus changing the targeted person's mood. More powerful beams of such energy could easily wreck the human nervous system permanently.[69] A growing number of investigators are convinced that the United States employed radio-frequency wave "mind control" weapons during certain phases of the Persian Gulf War.[70]

Internally, the human body communicates by electromagnetism (EM) and electrochemical impulses. Chinese acupuncture, Japanese shiatsu therapeutic massage, and the dreaded dim-mak all work by influencing the flow of our natural internal EM field, which is closely related to the Taoist concept of *chi*. It has been theorized that fluctuations of the body's EM field may be responsible for people experiencing various "psychic" phenomenon (seeing visions, ghosts, etc.).

This is not surprising considering that researchers have discovered that the deliberate manipulation of the body's EM field can actually cause such phenomenon.

In *People of theWeb*, Dr. Gregory Little explains how, like a hallucinogenic drug, EM fields can be used to alter brain chemistry and influence a person's perception of reality.[71]

At Laurentian University in Canada, neuropsychologist Michael Persinger designed a computer-controlled helmet (dubbed "the God Machine") which, by focusing small magnetic fields around the heads of test subjects, causes them to have "mystical" and "psychic" experiences (such as seeing visions or experiencing being abducted by a UFO). Such studies seem to indicate that many such experiences and phenomenon, rather than actually being caused by an external force, may be caused by over-stimulated neurochemical processes within the brain itself.[72]

The 1992 discovery of the mineral magnetite in the human brain provided a valuable link to how EM can influence the body and mind. Areas in the brain's temporal lobe are among the richest in receptors for endorphin (the brain's natural painkillers). It is this area of the brain that is most affected by magnetic fields, both the artificial EM field created by The God Machine, and by naturally-occurring geomagnetic fields radiating from the Earth.

Persinger suggests that exposure to such fields may act like LSD, triggering endorphins in the brain, and creating subjective "mystical experiences."

Imagine such a tool in the hands of a cult leader who could cause cult members to see visions anytime he wanted. Other mind-slayers might use this technology to make victim's believe they possess psychic abilities. Rogue government agencies might use the technology to convince sane individuals they are going crazy.

The fact that external EM conditions can affect a person's moods, for example influencing their susceptibility or resistance to new ideas, may validate belief in Eastern astrology. Simply put, the "base EM frequency" (caused by atmospheric EM variables and naturally-fluctuating EM fields of the Earth) in affect at the time of our birth could continue to influence us— positively or negatively—throughout our lives as that EM frequency fluctuates up and down due to external (and internal) factors. Such oscillations would affect our moods, our performance, etc.

The Ion Attackers

Negative ions (electrically charged atoms) in the air enhance alertness and create exhilaration. An excess of positive ions, on the other hand, produces drowsiness and depression. Devices are already being sold commercially that increase negative ions in a room. These devices are very popular with cult leaders and with other mind-slayers who use these devices to help "relax" potential victims, making them more susceptible to their message.

Beyond individual use, calculation of the ionic content of an enemy army's location can help determine that foe's level of readiness. Thus, the study of pre-battle weather conditions becomes all the more important.

On the more proactive side, devices are in development to allow the military to deliberately flood enemy-held territory with positive (pacifying) ions, sapping a foreign army (or domestic rioters) of their will to fight.

Such ion weapons fall into the category of "calmative agents," part of a growing arsenal of "non-lethal" police and military weapons designed to defeat foes without killing them.

When employed, these calmative agents are mixed with DMSO (which quickly delivers chemicals through the skin into the bloodstream).[73]

Killer Cartoons

"[The victors of WW II] introduced an all-pervasive, ultra-powerful society-shaping drug. This drug was the first of a growing group of high-technology drugs that deliver the user into an alternate reality by acting directly on the user's sensorium, without chemicals being introduced into the nervous system. It was television. No epidemic or addictive craze or religious hysteria has ever moved faster or made as many converts in so short a time."

—Terrence McKenna, *Food of the Gods*[74]

In Toyko, December 1997, more than 700 people, most of them children, were rushed to hospitals complaining of a host of ailments (ranging from blackouts to nausea, spasms, and hyperventilation) after watching the children's cartoon *Pokémon* (*Pocket Monsters*), based on a Nintendo game of the same name. Twenty minutes into the program there appeared scenes with strobing light producing "rhythmic bursts of blue, red, and white light" so intense it interrupted normal brain function.

Although aimed primarily at elementary school-aged children, victims of the seizures ranged from ages 3 to 20. Initially nearly 600 were effected, but the number rose to 729 after kids watched a videotaped rerun of the show. Other factors believed contributing to the seizures were the intense concentration with which young viewers normally watch the fast-paced show, and the fact that most of those affected lived in cramped apartments with large-screen TVs sitting only three feet away.

A normal brain functions by processing electrical impulses at regular rhythms, sort of like a telegraph sending Morse code. A strobe-like pulsing light flashing at a certain frequency can upset this "code," in effect, changing a "dot" here to a "dash" there; changing the message the brain receives from "get up" to "shut down," throwing the brain into a seizure.

After investigation, authorities declared the *Pokémon* incident to have been unintentional.

However, two years earlier in May 1995, Japan's infamous Aum Shunri Kyo "Supreme Truth" cult (responsible for the March 1995 Sarin nerve gas attack on Tokyo's subway that killed 12 and left 5,500 injured), slipped a subliminal picture of cult leader Shoko Asahara into another popular children's television show.[75]

Whatever you think of television, you would be foolish to dismiss it as a mindless boob tube. "Mind-controlling" might be a more apt description:

"Television is by nature the dominator drug par excellence. Control of content, uniformity of content, repeatability of content make it inevitably a tool of coercion, brainwashing, and manipulation. Television induces a trance state in the viewer that is the necessary precondition for brainwashing."[76]

Cults and others fully realize the potential of television. Television and videotapes can easily be paired with other psychotronic innovations such as subliminal VLF and pacifying ion sprays designed to make the viewer even more receptive to the small screen's magic.

According to a report in the July 1975 issue of *The American Journal of Clinical Hypnosis*, hypnotic induction by videotape is as effective as induction by a live person. This explains why modern religious and motivational cults require recruits to view endless hours of "The Leader" on videotape.

Blue Beam and Beyond

There are always two sides to any innovation, be that innovation philosophical or technological. New developments in technology can be used for good or to do harm, to heal or hurt.

While modern mind-slayers hone the powers of mind that nature gave them—and greed perverted—they are ever on the lookout for any new technology offering to make their edge all the more keen.

In order not to become the slave of such developments, it is important we keep up on the latest in psychotronics, especially since there is some scary stuff on the horizon:

Implants. In Michael Crichton's novel and subsequent movie *The Terminal Man*, emotion-controlling implants ("terminals") are placed in a violent man's brain to help him control his homicidal rage. This cautionary Frankenstein story ends predictably, with the implants burning out and the killer going berserk and slaughtering everybody connected with the project.

While the plot is fictional, the technology for implanting such devices in the human brain has been around since the 1960s. Only the medical community's precarious hold on ethics keeps them from using such a tool. Beware: Others are not constrained by the Hippocratic oath.

Some even believe we are not far from the day when computer links and other brain-enhancing devices will routinely be implanted in our brains and bodies, even as today hearing aids and heart pacemakers are implanted. With nanotechnology, microscopic machines capable of delivering drugs or a tiny, mood-altering EM pulse would be injected into the bloodstream (via a syringe or an "accidental" cut). From there, these tiny time bombs would make their way to the brain where they could lay dormant for years, waiting for their signal (a certain frequency, a spoken word) to activate.[77]

Virtual Reality. Cults routinely isolate their members in communes, artificial utopias where the recruit is kept "safe" from the wickedness of the outside world.

This is nothing new. In medieval Persia, the infamous Sect of the Assassins maintained a secret garden where drugged recruits would awaken to find their every fantasy fulfilled. Later these recruits would again be drugged and, upon awakening, find themselves back in the mundane world where they would be assured that if they died in the service of the cult, they would return to paradise. Having already seen heaven first-hand, such men became suicidal killing machines.[78]

Virtual reality (VR) has us on the threshold of creating electronically created environments where victims (such as cult recruits or captured POWs) could be "trapped" without their knowledge. With the current technology, an excursion into VR requires a traveler to wear a bulky helmet and special gloves that allow him to interact with the computer world. Yet the VR equipment of today is far less bulky than it was five years ago. Five years from now, it may disappear altogether, replaced by a VR room, or even by VR contact lenses.

In the worst-case scenario, we can envision a time in the not-too-distant future where an unwitting victim could become trapped in a VR world of his enemies' construction, never knowing he'd been captured—or perhaps given a taste of VR "heaven" as medieval Assassin recruits were hundreds of years ago.

Faking UFOs. UFOologist Jacques Vallee proposes that UFO phenomenon may actually be a secret form of psychotronic mind control.[79]

Likewise, author Robert Temple says that faking UFO abductions and even mass sightings could be accomplished through the use of sophisticated hypnotic procedures.[80] For example, highly suggestible subjects, chosen in advance, could be given a post-hypnotic suggestion that an "abduction" will occur at specific time and place.[81]

Once programmed, this post-hypnotic suggestion could be triggered by watching an innocuous television message or hearing a trigger word spoken over the phone. Hypnotized individuals might be programmed to arrive at the same place at the same time in order to "witness" such an event. Faking UFO encounters might also include dressing people as aliens (a là *The X-Files*).

Project Blue Beam. In 312, at the Battle of Milvian Bridge, Roman Emperor Constantine saw the vision of a bright cross hovering over the battlefield. This inspired him to win the battle and embrace Christianity, thus creating the Holy Roman Empire.

Other religious movers and shakers were also inspired by the appearance of heavenly signs. For example Joan of Arc (1412-1431) saw a vision of Mary commanding her to rally the French during the Hundred Years War. The apostle Paul was struck down on the road to Damascus by a brilliant light that inspired him to convert to the new Christian "cult." Mohammed received a vision of the angel Gabriel, founded Islam, and the rest is bloody history.

Whatever the truth of these historical visions, there is no denying the world-shaking events that often follow such "revelations." Today, the technology exists to fake such heavenly—or devilish—events.

In his comprehensive report *Project Blue Beam*, Canadian journalist Serge Monast investigated a United States government study into the feasibility of using holographs as weapons. Monast died shortly after making this information public.

The simplest way to explain a holograph is that criss-crossing laser beams create a 3-D image capable of being seen from all angles. This technology opens the possibility of projecting images into the sky in order to affect the minds of anyone seeing the images. Even on a small scale, cult leaders could make "angels" or "devils" appear.

On a larger scale, a Middle Eastern tyrant might cause a Godlike hand to appear, writing verses from the Koran calling for Jihad (Holy War) over the heads of his waiting army. Might those Muslims then fight to the death? This kind of sky show could be used in connection with "electronic telepathy," using ELF, VLF, and LF waves, beaming messages directly into onlookers' brains, making them believe God was sending them messages.

Or what if the government decided to fake an alien invasion?

As early as 1917, Professor John Dewy (member of Britain's elitist Fabian Socialist society) stated that the best way to unite Earth would be an alien threat.

This was not the last time a "common world threat" solution was proposed.

Some maintain that Orson Welles' infamous *War of the Worlds* radio broadcast that panicked listeners in 1939 was a government dry-run, testing the public's readiness should such an emergency announcement (real or rigged) have to be used.

At the 1963 Iron Mountain summit of the Kennedy administration's Special Study Group, it was again proposed that faking an "alien invasion" was a viable alternative for war.

One theory behind the sudden resolution of the October 1962 Cuban Missile Crisis was that, in order to avert war with the Soviets, Kennedy convinced the Soviets they shared a "common threat" by showing the Soviets the crashed flying saucer recovered at Roswell, New Mexico, in 1949.

For conspiracy buffs, the ultimate Blue Beam scenario has been dubbed "The Night of 1,000 Stars": It will begin with phony earthquakes, predicted ahead of time by "psychics" on trash-talk TV, psychics either in the pay of the government or else individuals targeted for subliminal (EM) messages. A campaign to debunk traditional religions (Christianity, Islam, etc.) would already be in place (in media, movies, etc). This disinformation campaign would be further aided by new "scientific discoveries" (in the fields of archeology and astronomy) calling religious scriptures into question.

This program would culminate in gigantic "signs in the sky" produced by lasers. One scenario has traditional religious figures (Jesus, Mohammed,

Krishna, and Buddha) appearing in the sky and then merging into form one new God!

A liberal use of ELF, VLF, and LF subliminal waves would make people "hear" this new God speaking directly to them inside their heads.

An already-in-place Emergency Broadcasting System computer chip that turns your television on automatically whenever there is a national emergency would allow images to be projected along existing fiber-optic lines, causing "angels" (or aliens) to appear in your living room. Amidst the chaos that follows, the government is "forced" to declare martial law and suspend civil rights.

People pray to the "New Messiah" to deliver them and he does, giving his blessing to specific leaders or to the "New World Order."

Far-fetched? All the technology for a "Blue Beam" scenario exists today, whether for targeting masses of people or for singling out individuals for shadowy purposes.

Submitted for your approval: On March 13, 1997, thousands of Phoenix, Arizona, citizens watched while a "V-shaped object, three football fields long" hovered 6,000 feet above the city for 106 minutes. Although this UFO was videotaped from several angles, it failed to show up on radar.

The air force dismissed the phenomenon as flares dropped by passing aircraft.

Even using such psychotronic technology on an individual (a potential Joan of Arc or a wannabe Mohammed) could have far-reaching consequence. Consider:

At a press conference held in Washington, D.C. in October 1989, and subsequently repeated in the November 30, 1989, issue of the Nation of Islam's newspaper *The Final Call*, Louis Farrakhan claimed that on the night of September 17, 1985, while on a hilltop near ancient ruins in Tepotzlan, Mexico, he was lifted up by a UFO "wheel" and carried to a gigantic "Mother Wheel" in orbit above the Earth.

This Mother Wheel was 1 / 2 mile by 1 / 2 mile in size.

According to Farrakhan, this gigantic spaceship was built by humans and is the same "Mother Plane" preached about by Farrakhan's predecessor Elijah Muhammed, founder of The Nation of Islam. Farrakhan said that while on this ship he heard the voice of the dead Elijah Muhammed speaking to him.

Three possible explanations have been proposed for Farrakhan's vision:

First, Farrakhan made the whole thing up in order to more closely link himself in his followers' minds with the mythology of a gigantic Mother Plane spaceship espoused by his predecessor. Or, Farrakhan really had such a vision, a dream springing from his own wish-fulfillment. The brain tends to see what it wants to see. Finally, and perhaps most ominously, many believe Farrakhan was the victim of a Blue Beam-type operation, either in order to discredit him, or in order to manipulate him toward a specific agenda.

"It is conceivable that the Image of the Beast could be a laser holographic image or perhaps a robot that New Age priests and ministers someday will set up in churches and temples throughout the world."[82]

Ninja learned long ago that any weapon, no matter how technologically advanced, is only an extension of their own mind and body, their senses and savvy.[83]

Mind-slayers—whether they be individuals or belong to cults or governments—all keep up on the latest psychotronic weapons in order to further their own shadowy agenda.

We would therefore be remiss if we did not do likewise, if only for safety and sanity's sake.

To allow fear of technology to prevent us from keeping abreast of the latest science would be foolish, when we will undoubtedly benefit from future technology as we have past developments. However, we must never forget that a good knife cuts both ways:

"For the sword of knowledge cuts two ways. It can be used in offense. It can destroy an opponent even before his first lunge. But it can also cut off the very hand that wields it."[84]

MIND-DANCING

Kamiizumi Hidetsuna, 16th century samurai founder of the *shinkage-ryu* of ninjutsu ("New Shade School," so-called for the "shade" pulled over a foe's eyes) once saved a hostage child from a sword-wielding madman by using a single rice cake.

Rather than physically trying to overpower the lunatic and risk further endangering the child, Kamiizumi opted to "mind-dance" around the enraged man.

Disguising himself as a Buddhist monk, Kamiizumi slowly approached the madman and his hostage, offering the child a rice cake and then tossing one to the madman. When the madman instinctively reached to catch the rice cake, Kamiizumi grabbed hold of the madman's extended arm and easily restrained him with a jujutsu hold.

Kamiizumi's "mind-dance" employed the following insights:

First, by donning the guise of a Buddhist monk, Kamiizumi invoked the man's social conditioning, that is, the respect all Japanese are taught for a holy man.

Second, it is universally known that Buddhist monks are sworn to peace, therefore the madman did not feel threatened by the harmless monk approaching.

Third, Kamiizumi recognized that the enraged man was functioning on a primal rage level. To try reasoning on a higher level with such a person would be useless and only confuse him all the more.

Therefore, Kamiizumi opted to meet the man on the same level at which the lunatic was functioning, distracting the madman with an even more basic urge, hunger. Finally, tossing the rice cakes reveals Kamiizumi's knowledge of instinctive body reactions.

An interviewer once asked Bruce Lee to describe the "essence" of Lee's martial arts. In response, Lee threw an apple to the interviewer who reacted by instinctively by catching it. "That, is the essence of my art!" Lee explained, indicating the natural action the interviewer had performed without conscious thought.

To the average person mind-dancing sounds exotic, yet mastery of psychological warfare—defensive or offensive, on the battlefield or in the boardroom—brings us one step closer to Sun Tzu's ideal of subduing an enemy without fighting.

Guarding your Mind Castle

As we said earlier, think of yourself as a castle. The physical walls are your actual body and its innermost locked and guarded rooms are your mind. The gates, windows, and other openings in a castle allow a ninja to spy on what is going on inside the castle and to enter that stronghold by stealth.

In the same way, our everyday actions and reactions, as well as our five senses, are the gates, windows, and all-too-easily jimmied doors through which a wily mind-slayer slips in unnoticed.

From our study of body language, we know our actions (conscious and unconscious) can give others insight into our thinking. Our physical stumblings and verbal slip-ups are windows into our minds, through which can be glimpsed our deeper (perhaps deliberately hidden, perhaps subconsciously buried) fears and desires.

In addition to our observable actions, there are nine "gates" into our mind castle, as we discussed in Chapter 2. These gates are the nine openings in the body: eyes, ears, nostrils, mouth, urethra (organs of sex), and the anus. While we diligently guard our castle's drawbridge (the conscious mind), adept mind-slayers slip in through one of these unguarded gates.

Over the centuries, many ingenious ploys have been developed by mind-slayers to penetrate these nine gates. Often the mind-slayer penetrates our mind castle below our line of sight (the way a ninja burglar might enter a stronghold through a neglected drain or unguarded sewer) by attacking us obliquely, through our friends and families.

Or, no matter what guards we stand atop the walls, these spies of the mind walk boldly in the front door disguised as a trusted friend, a priest, or a salesman with an offer too good to turn down.

In other words, eyes can easily be dazzled and ears seduced by hearing what they want to hear. "Sweet-smelling" offers, like the richest of perfumes, can literally lead us around by the nose. Likewise our various appetites and our sex drive can be targeted by a skilled mind-slayer.

Bypassing Defense Mechanisms

To guard our own mind castles, we construct and maintain elaborate defense mechanisms; strong-arm strategies and avoidance tactics designed to keep out unwanted visitors.

The particular defense mechanism an individual favors tells the mind-slayer much about that person's personality. There are basically three types of defense ploys: avoidance, rationalizing, and anger.

Avoidance Ploys

Avoidance ploys are either active or passive. Active avoidance includes distraction (including flattery, vague generalizing, joking about serious matters, and attention-shifting humor) and distancing (pushing people away by being obnoxious or by giving them the silent treatment, and the geographic cure, simply running away from problems, for example to a bar or a cult).

Sex can also be used to avoid facing problems, a way to both change the subject (distracting) and to temporarily change the way you feel (distancing).

Passive-avoidance defenses include pretending to be helpless (a sympathy ploy), self-depreciation (putting oneself down in order to avoid taking responsibility), being lazy, and shifting the blame to others.

Lying and cheating can be both passive and active.

Rationalizing Ploys

Rationalizing ploys include minimizing (downplaying the extent of a problem), slow-walking (drawing out a problem by talking it to death), and justifying (making excuses for your actions and the actions of others).

Anger Ploys

Anger Ploys can be directed outward or turned inward.

Outward-directed anger appears as sarcasm, snitching, making faulty comparisons ("You do it, too!"), maximizing (blowing things out of proportion), verbal abuse, vandalism, and violence. Anger turned inward shows up as self-pity, feelings of powerlessness, fear of success (anxiety over being given added responsibility), recklessness, and self-destruction (unconsciously sabotaging yourself, deliberate self-mutilation, or suicide). (Note: Anger is almost always a secondary emotion used to cover a primary feeling.)

When confronted with unexpected and/or inappropriate anger, mind-slayers seek the real cause, for example a hidden fear or secret desire that is not being satisfied. Having discovered this true source of the person's anger and frustration, the mind-slayer institutes a two-step attack: commiserate and satiate. That is, tell the victim you understand and offer him a way to satisfy his needs.

"Over the Wall!"

A masterful military commander will never attack an enemy blindly, not without first gathering every piece of intelligence about that enemy's weaknesses and blind spots.

To map out his attack strategy, a commander uses information drawn from many sources, including intelligence brought him from spies and traitors in the enemy camp.

In the same way, adroit mind-slayers use their abilities to spot our favored defense mechanisms to help them map out their strategies prior to beginning their assaults on our mind castles.

Once the mind-slayer has figured out a person's favored defense mechanism(s), the mind-slayer then adds fuel to the fire by encouraging that defense mechanism. Even though these defense mechanisms are inherently bad for the person clinging to them, the ruthless mind-slayer assures his victim that his way of dealing with life is perfect. Perfect, that is, for the mind-slayer!

Since everyone else (family, friends, counselors) keeps begging the victim to change, the mind-slayer (in his guise of confidant, cult leader, or fellow gang member) assures the victim that he or she is right and everyone else is wrong. This further endears the mind-slayer to the victim, allowing the mind-slayer to get even closer.

Cults, fringe political groups, and disenfranchised ethnic groups often collectively adopt these same defense mechanisms as part of their shared group identity.

Maslow's Pyramid

Buddha taught that wanting things we don't need is the beginning of all suffering. Yet all of us have things we need in order to survive.

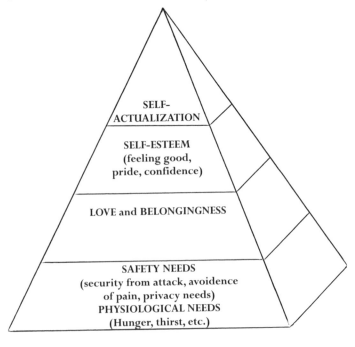

SELF-
ACTUALIZATION

SELF-ESTEEM
(feeling good,
pride, confidence)

LOVE and BELONGINGNESS

SAFETY NEEDS
(security from attack, avoidence
of pain, privacy needs)
PHYSIOLOGICAL NEEDS
(Hunger, thirst, etc.)

Psychologist Abraham Maslow (1908-1970) is famous for summing up a basic list of human needs and priorities in what has become known simply as "Maslow's Pyramid."

At the most basic level all of us have physical needs (food, sleep, sex) and safety needs (protection, freedom from fear, a need for familiar and reassuring structure in our lives).

Once these basic physical and safety needs are satisfied, we turn our attention to the second tier of the pyramid, needs for love and a sense of belonging.

Self-esteem needs (a need to feel vital and valued) and self-actualization needs (the need to explore one's full potential) top off Maslow's Pyramid.

Where a person focuses on this pyramid of needs determines their priorities. Determining a person's priorities then enables the mind-slayer to either encourage that person's negative priorities, or stifle his positive priorities.

****

Some say honest people shouldn't study these techniques of mind-manipulation, that it is truly "The Black Science."

Yet what is blacker, this dark craft to be mastered—or the blackness of the grave planned for us by mind-slayers if we decline to learn The Black Science?

ENDNOTES

1. Lung, Haha. *Assassin! Secrets of the Cult of Assassins*. Boulder, Colorado: Paladin Press, 1997.

2. Lung, Haha. *The Ancient Art of Strangulation*. Boulder, Colorado: Paladin Press, 1995.

3. Davis, Wade. *The Serpent and the Rainbow*. New York: Simon and Schuster, 1985.

4. John Stossel, *The Power of Belief*. ABC-TV. Original air date: October 6, 1998.

5. Omar, Ralf Dean. *Ninja Death Touch: The Fact and the Fiction*. *Black Belt* magazine, September, 1989.

6. Corsini, Raymond J., editor. Encyclopedia of Psychology. New York: Wiley, 1984.

7. Hare, Robert D. *Without Conscience: the Disturbing World of the Psychopaths Among Us*. New York: Pocket Books, 1993.

8. New York Times News Service, June 16, 1996.

9. Skinner, B.F. *A Matter of Consequences*. New York: Knopf, 1983.

10. Lung, Haha. *The Ancient Art of Strangulation*. Boulder, Colorado: Paladin Press, 1995.

11. Hare, Robert D. *Without Conscience: the Disturbing World of the Psychopaths Among Us*. New York: Pocket Books, 1993.

12. Sifakis, Carl. *Encyclopedia of American Crime*. New York: Facts-on-File, 1981.
13. *USA Today* March 6, 1992.
14. Regardie, Israel. *The Tree of Life: A Study in Magic*. New York: Samuel Weiser Co., 1994.
15. Holzer, Hans. *ESP and You*. New York: Hawthorn Books, 1966.
16. Sifakis, Carl. *Encyclopedia of American Crime*. New York: Facts-on-File, 1981.
17. *USA Today*. January 29, 1992
18. *USA Today*. April 17, 1992.
19. Sifakis, Carl. *Encyclopedia of American Crime*. New York: Facts-on-File, 1981.
20. Ibid.
21. Ibid.
22. Ibid.
23. *L.A. Times*. March 25, 1995.
24. Singer, Margaret Thaler. *Cults in our Midst*. San Francisco: Jossey-Bass Publishers, 1995.
25. Loftus, Elizabeth F. and Katherine Ketcham. *The Myth of Repressed Memory: False Memories and Allegations of Sexual Abuse*. New York: St. Martin's Press, 1994.
26. Bain, Donald. The Control of Candy Jones. Chicago: Playboy Press, 1976.
27. Bain, Donald. The Control of Candy Jones. Chicago: Playboy Press, 1976.
28. Bain, Donald. The Control of Candy Jones. Chicago: Playboy Press, 1976.
29. Little, G.L. *Spectral Intrusions Part VII: The Geomagnetic Explanation. Alternate Perceptions*, Winter 1997.
30. O'Brien, Cathy with Mark Phillips. *Trance Formation of America*. Las Vegas, Nev.: Reality Marketing, 1995.
31. Morehouse, David. *Psychic Warrior: Inside the CIA's Stargate Program*. New York: St. Martin's Press, 1996.
32. *Strange Universe*. November 12, 1997
33. Jones, Ron. *The Third Wave*. The Next Whole Earth Catalog, 1980.
34. Thio, Alex. *Sociology: A Brief Introduction*. New York: HarperCollins College Publishers, 1994.
35. Zimbardo, Philip G. *The Psychology of Police Confessions. Psychology Today*, June 1967.
36. *USA TODAY*. June 1, 1995.
37. Loftus, Elizabeth F. and Katherine Ketcham. *The Myth of Repressed Memory: False Memories and Allegations of Sexual Abuse*. New York: St. Martin's Press, 1994.
38. *Newsweek*. April 4, 1994.
39. Kadish, Sanford H. editor in chief. *Encyclopedia of Crime and Justice*. New York: Free Press, 1983.
40. KUBARK Counterintelligence Interrogation, CIA training manual, July 1963.
41. Holzer, Hans. *ESP and You*. New York: Hawthorn Books, 1966.
42. Zimbardo, Philip G. *The Psychology of Police Confessions. Psychology Today*, June 1967.
43. KUBARK Counter Intelligence Interrogation, CIA training manual, July 1963.
44. Kadish, Sanford H. editor in chief. *Encyclopedia of Crime and Justice*. New York: Free Press, 1983.
45. Sifakis, Carl. *Encyclopedia of American Crime*. New York: Facts-on-File, 1981.

46. Bain, Donald. *The Control of Candy Jones.* Chicago: Playboy Press, 1976.

47. Sills, David L. editor. *International Encyclopedia of the Social Sciences.* New York: Macmillan, 1968, Vol. 12.

48. Holzer, Hans. *ESP and You.* New York: Hawthorn Books, 1966.

49. Sills, David L. editor. *International Encyclopedia of the Social Sciences.* New York: Macmillan, 1968, Vol. 12.

50. Ibid.

51. Goldenson, Robert M. *The Encyclopedia of Human Behavior.* Garden City, New York: Doubleday, 1970.

52. Holzer, Hans. *ESP and You.* New York: Hawthorn Books, 1966.

53. Toffler, Alvin and Heidi Toffler. *War and Anti-War: Survival at the Dawn of the 21st Century.* New York: Little, Brown & Company, 1993.

54. Ringer, Robert J. *Winning Through Intimidation.* Crest/Fawcett, 1993.

55. Sills, David L. editor. *International Encyclopedia of the Social Sciences.* New York: Macmillan, 1968, Vol. 12.

56. Tripodi, Tom and Joseph P. DeSario. *Crusade: Undercover against the Mafia and KGB.* Brassey's, 1992.

57. Goldenson, Robert M. *The Encyclopedia of Human Behavior.* Garden City, New York: Doubleday, 1970.

58. Sills, David L. editor. *International Encyclopedia of the Social Sciences.* New York: Macmillan, 1968, Vol. 12.

59. Few people know that William M. Marston, the man credited with inventing the modern polygraph machine (lie-detector) was also the creator of the comic book character Wonder Woman (using his pen-name, Charles Moulton).

60. Zeman, Zbynek. A.B. *Nazi Propaganda.* London, New York: Oxford University Press, 1973.

61. Ibid.

62. Drosnin, Michael. *Mind Control in Waco? Village Voice,* March 8, 1994.

63. Ibid.

64. Elliot, D. and J. Barry. *A Subliminal Dr. Strangelove. Newsweek,* August 22, 1994.

65. Drosnin, Michael. *Mind Control in Waco? Village Voice,* March 8, 1994.

66. Clarke, Arthur C. *July 20, 2019: Life in the 21st Century.* New York: Mcmillan, 1986.

67. Ibid.

68. Toffler, Alvin and Heidi Toffler. *War and Anti-War: Survival at the Dawn of the 21st Century.* New York: Little, Brown & Company, 1993.

69. *Vancouver Sun.* January 25, 1992.

70. "Weapons of the Future Attack the Mind," *Sunshine Coast Daily,* February 27, 1993.

71. Little, Gregory. *People of the Web.* Memphis, TN: White Buffalo Books, 1990.

72. Ibid.

73. Toffler, Alvin and Heidi Toffler. *War and Anti-War: Survival at the Dawn of the 21st Century.* New York: Little, Brown & Company, 1993.

74. McKenna, Terrence. *Food of the Gods: The Search for the Original Tree of Knowledge: A Radical*

History of Plants, Drugs, and Human Evolution. New York: Bantam Books, 1992.

75. *USA Today*, May 30, 1995.
76. McKenna, Terrence. *Food of the Gods: The Search for the Original Tree of Knowledge: A Radical History of Plants, Drugs, and Human Evolution*. New York: Bantam Books, 1992.
77. Toffler, Alvin and Heidi Toffler. *War and Anti-War: Survival at the Dawn of the 21st Century*. New York: Little, Brown & Company, 1993.
78. Lung, Haha. *Assassin! Secrets of the Cult of Assassins*. Boulder, Colorado: Paladin Press, 1997.
79. Vallee, Jacques. *Messengers of Deception: UFO Contacts and Cults*. Berkeley, Calif.: And/Or Press, 1979.
80. Temple, Robert. The Sirius Mystery. London: Sidgwick and Jackson, 1976.
81. Sachs, Margaret. *The UFO Encyclopedia*. New York: Putnam, 1980.
82. Marrs, Texe. *Mystery Mark of the New Age: Satan's Design for World Domination*. Westchester, Illinois: Crossway Books, 1988.
83. Skinner, Dirk. *Street Ninja: Ancient Secrets for Surviving Today's Mean Streets*. New York: Barricade Books, 1995.
84. Toffler, Alvin and Heidi Toffler. *War and Anti-War: Survival at the Dawn of the 21st Century*. New York: Little, Brown & Company, 1993.

CONCLUSION

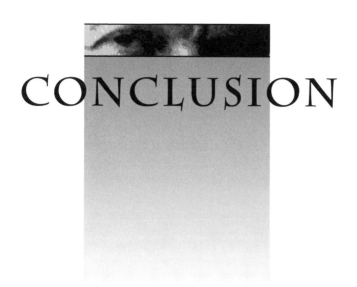

Make a man hungry enough and he will eat out of your hand.

Make him fearful and he will long for security and gladly hand you the keys to his front door.

Deprive him of comfort, sex, and a feeling of self-worth and he will listen to any plan—no matter how outrageous—to get them back.

Frustrate him and otherwise unsettle him and even the deadliest of trained killers will make the foolish, fatal mistakes of the amateur.

Madison Avenue mind-slayers make us think we can't live without the latest car—the one the bikini-clad babe is leaning on. Government mind-slayers send forth daily the enthusiastic naive to die in "wag-the-dog" misadventures. Mind-slayer cultists routinely attract the disaffected and the insecure with open arms of acceptance and promises of power over enemies.

Use or be used is the rule when it comes to dealing with these mind-slayers. Arm yourself with knowledge or ever remain victim and eventual slave to mind-slayers so armed.

In the end, we have only two options: learn the ways of the ruthless mind-slayer better than he knows those ways himself, thus turning the tables on him. Or, bury our heads in the sand like ostriches and try to wish all the mind-slayers in the world away—or at least wish that they would pick on someone else.

Prudently, let us choose to study their ways.

Even if you bury your head in the sand, you can still get your ass kicked!

GLOSSARY

Amettori-jutsu: Literally, "a man of straw." Encompasses all tactics and techniques of deception. The name comes from the ploy of dressing up a scarecrow to make an enemy think it is a real sentry or soldier.

Cutting at the edges: Undermining another's confidence by eroding his "comfort-zone."

Dim-mak: Death touch

Ekkyo: Divination methods that allow us to determine a victim's birth order and examine their interactions with others, especially close relatives.

Gojo-goyoku: "Five Element Theory." Derived from the Chinese pseudo-science of wu-hsing, which teaches that all reality (including actions and attitudes) is composed of five basic forces: earth, air, fire, water, and void. In all things and all times, one of these elements is dominant. Each element has a corresponding element in opposition to it.

In-yo-jutsu: Tactics designed to "unbalance" an opponent, to sow doubt and distrust in his mind.

Jodomon: "The way of the cat." Individuals who take this approach depend on tariki ("another's power").

Jomon-jutsu: The use of special words and phrases designed to affect an individual's emotional stability, for example words evoking fear, lust, or patriotism.

Jujushin: Identifies "10 Minds," or 10 levels of understanding and functioning into which human beings can be categorized.

Junishi-do-jutsu: Employing the ancient art of Chinese astrology to determine a person's overall temperament as well as his weakest time of the day, when he is most susceptible to physical attack and mental manipulation.

Kami: Evil spirits.

Kiai-shin-jutsu: Tactics and techniques that directly attack the intended victim psychologically by "shouting" into his mind.

Kuniochi: A female ninja.

Kyonin-no-jutsu: The art of using another's beliefs and superstitions against him.

Makoto: "The stainless mind." Makoto is a balanced state of mind allowing us to remain calm even in the most trying of circumstance. The development of makoto consists of the active cultivation and practice of two skills: haragei (awareness), and rinkioken (adaptability).

Mind-dancing: psychological warfare.

One-Eyed Snake: This strategy was comprised of tactics and techniques intended to give outsiders the illusion the ninja possessed true magical powers, in particular, the power to strike down a foe from afar and/or with a single touch without so much as a mark left on the victim

Pakua: The "eight trigrams." Pakua are eight symbols, consisting of three lines each. Each symbol represents one of eight basic relationships and interactions of life.

Ronin: A masterless samurai.

Satsujin-jutsu: Insights into the minds or natures of men.

Seishinshugi: Literally "mind over matter."

Sennin: Mind masters.

Seppuku: Ritual suicide.

Shodomon: "The way of the monkey," depends on jiriki ("one's own strength"). Individuals with this approach to life are independent; journeying alone, finding their own way; keeping their own counsel; and binding their own wounds—both physically and psychically. On the one extreme, these kinds of people are rugged individualists. At the opposite extreme, they are stubborn isolationists and control freaks, unable to take another's counsel.

Tengu demons: Either black or red in color, they are master shape-shifters. When appearing in human form, they appear as little men wearing short cloaks (made of feathers, leaves, or straw) and wearing large black hats. Tengu were great swordsmen and possessed powers of magic and invisibility. Shinobi ninja convinced their superstitious enemies that they were descended from the tengu.

The 10 Minds: Buddhists use each of the "10 Minds" (jujushin) as stepping stones to enlightenment. For ninja mind-slayers, on the other hand, the jujushin was just another stumbling block to place in the path of a foe. These Ten Minds are: Goat's Mind, Fool's Mind, Child's Mind, Dead Man's Mind, No-Karma Mind, Compassionate Mind, Unborn Mind; Single-Truth Mind, No-Self Mind, and Secret Mind. Each of the 10 Minds contains the seed of the others.

Wa: Your spirit, presence, or intention.

Wu-sing: "The Five Movers." This concept maintains that all reality is made up of five basic elements: earth (chi); air (fu); fire (la); water (sui); and void (ku).

Yugen-shin-jutsu: Literally "mysterious mind," uses various methods of hypnotism and subliminal suggestion to influence and control the minds of others.

Zen-zone: That level of functioning where stainless mental awareness (makoto) and physical awareness merge, allowing us to instantly and effortlessly adapt to rapidly shifting circumstance.

SOURCES AND SUGGESTED READING

"Weapons of the Future Attack the Mind," *Sunshine Coast Daily*, February 27, 1993.

Bain, Donald. *The Control of Candy Jones*. Chicago: Playboy Press, 1976.

Clarke, Arthur C. *July 20, 2019: Life in the 21st Century*. New York: Mcmillan, 1986.

Corsini, Raymond J. *Encyclopedia of Psychology*. New York: Wiley, 1984

Davis, Wade. *The Serpent and the Rainbow*. New York: Simon and Schuster, 1985.

Drosnin, Michael. *Mind Control in Waco? Village Voice*, March 8, 1994.

Elliot, D. and J. Barry. *A Subliminal Dr. Strangelove. Newsweek*, August 22, 1994.

Goldenson, Robert M. *The Encyclopedia of Human Behavior*. Garden City, New York: Doubleday, 1970.

Hare, Robert D. *Without Conscience: the Disturbing World of the Psychopaths Among Us*. New York: Pocket Books, 1993.

Holzer, Hans. *ESP and You*. New York: Hawthorn Books, 1966.

Hooper, Judith and Dick Teresi. *The Three-Pound Universe*. New York: Macmillan, 1986.

Jones, Ron. *The Third Wave*. The Next Whole Earth Catalog, 1980.

Kadish, Sanford H. editor in chief. *Encyclopedia of Crime and Justice*. New York: Free Press, 1983.

Kama Sutra, The (misc. trans.)

Kaplan, David E., and Alec Dubro. *Yakuza: The Explosive Account of Japan's Criminal Underworld*. Reading, Mass.: Addison-Wesley, 1986

KUBARK Counterintelligence Interrogation, CIA training manual, July 1963.

Little, G.L. *Spectral Intrusions Part VII: The Geomagnetic Explanation. Alternate Perceptions*, Winter 1997.

Little, Gregory. *People of the Web*. Memphis, TN: White Buffalo Books, 1990.

Loftus, Elizabeth F. and Katherine Ketcham. *The Myth of Repressed Memory: False Memories and Allegations of Sexual Abuse*. New York: St. Martin's Press, 1994.

Lung, Haha. Dr. *Assassin! Secrets of the Cult of Assassins*. Boulder, Colorado: Paladin Press, 1997.

Lung, Haha. Dr. *Knights of Darkness*. Boulder, Colorado: Paladin Press, 1998.

Lung, Haha. Dr. *The Ancient Art of Strangulation*. Boulder, Colorado: Paladin Press, 1995.

Lung, Haha. Dr. *The Ninja Craft*. Boulder, Colorado: Paladin Press, 1997.

Marrs, Texe. *Mystery Mark of the New Age: Satan's Design for World Domination*. Westchester, Illinois: Crossway Books, 1988.

Marshall, Richard. *Mysteries of the Unexplained*. Pleasantville, NY: Reader's Digest Association, 1982

McKenna, Terrence. *Food of the Gods: The Search for the Original Tree of Knowledge: A Radical History of Plants, Drugs, and Human Evolution*. New York: Bantam Books, 1992.

Morehouse, David. *Psychic Warrior: Inside the CIA's Stargate Program*. New York: St. Martin's Press, 1996.

Musashi Miyamoto *A Book of Five Rings* (Misc. trans.)

O'Brien, Cathy with Mark Phillips. *Trance Formation of America*. Las Vegas, Nev.: Reality Marketing, 1995.

Omar, Ralf Dean. "Ninja Death Touch: The Fact and the Fiction." *Black Belt*, September, 1989.

Omar, Ralf Dean. *Death on Your Doorstep: 101 Weapons in the Home*. Ohio: Alpha Publications, 1993

Orwell, George. *1984*. New York: Harcourt, 2000.

Piaget, Gerald W. Ph.D. *Control Freaks: Who They Are and How to Stop Them from Running Your Life*. New York: Doubleday, 1991.

Regardie, Israel. *The Tree of Life: A Study in Magic*. New York: Samuel Weiser Co., 1994.

Ringer, Robert J. *Winning Through Intimidation*. Crest/Fawcett, 1993.

Sachs, Margaret. *The UFO Encyclopedia*. New York: Putnam, 1980.

Sifakis, Carl. *Encyclopedia of American Crime*. New York: Facts-on-File, 1981.

Sills, David L. editor. *International Encyclopedia of the Social Sciences*. New York: Macmillan, 1968, Vol. 12.

Singer, Margaret Thaler. *Cults in our Midst*. San Francisco: Jossey-Bass Publishers, 1995.

Skinner, B.F. *A Matter of Consequences*. New York: Knopf, 1983.

Skinner, Dirk. *Street Ninja: Ancient Secrets for Surviving Today's Mean Streets*. New York: Barricade Books, 1995.

Stossel, John. *The Power of Belief*. ABC-TV. Original air date: October 6, 1998.

Strange Universe. November 12, 1997.

Sun Tzu, *Ping Fa (Art of War)* (Misc. trans.)

Temple, Robert. *The Sirius Mystery*. London: Sidgwick and Jackson, 1976.

Thio, Alex. *Sociology: A Brief Introduction*. New York: HarperCollins College Publishers, 1994.

Toffler, Alvin and Heidi Toffler. *War and Anti-War: Survival at the Dawn of the 21st Century*. New York: Little, Brown & Company, 1993.

Tripodi, Tom and Joseph P. DeSario. *Crusade: Undercover against the Mafia and KGB*. Brassey's, 1992.

Vallee, Jacques. *Messengers of Deception: UFO Contacts and Cults*. Berkeley, Calif.: And/Or Press, 1979.

Zeman, Zbynek.A.B. *Nazi Propaganda*. London, New York: Oxford University Press, 1973.

Zimbardo, Philip G. *The Psychology of Police Confessions*. *Psychology Today*, June 1967.

ABOUT THE AUTHORS

Christopher B. Prowant is a noted researcher, author, and martial artist. He holds a black belt in zendokan-ryu taijutsu and a teaching degree in wan tsu hu chuan (tiger-style kung-fu).

Dr. Haha Lung is the author of more than a dozen books on martial arts and the mysterious cults of the East, including *The Ancient Art of Strangulation*, *Assassin!*, *Knights of Darkness*, and *Shadowhand*, all published by Paladin Press.

If you liked this book, you will also want to read these:

SHADOWHAND
The History and Secrets of Ninja Taisavaki
by Dr. Haha Lung and Christopher B. Prowant

Study the devastating techniques of stealth, secrecy and subterfuge Japan's shinobi ninja "shadowhanders" collected, honed and practiced to strike down their enemies. Plus learn to apply the strategies and tactics of ninja taisavaki to disguise your intention and misdirect the enemy's attention. 5 1/2 x 8 1/2, softcover, illus.,160 pp. **#10011344**

THE FIGHTING EDGE
Using Your Martial Arts to Fight Better
by James LaFond

What is it like to be in a real fight? What about the various martial arts claims – are they valid? James LaFond has more than 25 years experience as a martial artist, boxer and laborer in one of America's toughest cities. Learn from someone who deals with violence on a daily basis how to use your martial arts to become a smarter fighter. 5 1/2 x 8 1/2, softcover, 288 pp. **#10011302**

KOBUDO AND BUGEI
The Ancient Weapon Way of Okinawa and Japan
by Sid Campbell

Karate pioneer Sid Campbell bridges the gap between the bloody role of martial arts weapons on the ancient battlefields of Okinawa and Japan and their use in sparring competition today. Learn how to harness the rhythm of combat, "move in the shadows" during a match, employ clever deception tactics and much more. 8 1/2 x 11, softcover, photos, 96 pp. **#10009769**

FIGHTING POWER
How to Develop Explosive Punches, Kicks, Blocks, and Grappling
by Loren Christensen

Find out how to combine the latest techniques with centuries-old secrets, resistance exercises and proper body mechanics to make your punches, kicks, blocks and throws more powerful, as well as to defend yourself against explosive power. Double your fighting power by following this proven training regimen. 5 1/2 x 8 1/2, softcover, photos, 248 pp. **#10005759**

SPEED TRAINING
How to Develop Your Maximum Speed for Martial Arts
by Loren Christensen

Speed is the most important asset a fighter can have. Find out from a top martial artist and police officer how to develop instantaneous reflexes and explosive speed for punching, kicking, grappling and police defensive tactics. Improve perception, polish timing and double your speed by using these surefire techniques. 5 1/2 x 8 1/2, softcover, photos, 256 pp.**#10005387**